Language Teaching in Grades 1 and 2

REVISED EDITION

by Mildred A. Dawson

WORLD BOOK COMPANY

YONKERS-ON-HUDSON, NEW YORK

Acknowledgments

For permission to reprint copyrighted material, grateful acknowledgment is made to the following publishers and authors:

Expression Company: "The Nursery Clock," by Louise Abney, from *Choral Speaking Arrangements for the Lower Grades*, by Louise Abney.

World Book Company: Selected rhymes from *This Way to Better Speech*, by Louise Abney and Dorothy Miniace.

Table of Contents

The Language Program and the Child

Among the various factors that determine the general nature of the language program, possibly the most important are the characteristics of growing children, the influence of the social environment that surrounds them, and the nature of the modern school curriculum with its governing purposes and interrelationships. Chapter 1 will treat in considerable detail the influence of each of these three factors on the language curriculum in the early school years.

Children in the Early School Years

On the basis of experience at home and frequently in the kindergarten, the child enters the first grade with a considerable background in language. He has learned to listen comprehensively to directions and explanations as well as to stories, discussion, and conversation. At the same time, he has developed some ability to express himself in these ways. He has acquired a fairly good vocabulary, and he can organize words into sentences. Most of the words he speaks are articulated with reasonable correctness and clarity as he relates an experience, poses a multitude of questions, gives directions to a companion, engages in dramatic play, repeats a favorite rhyme, or tells a story.

1

Preschool Vocabulary and Language Ability   It is probable that the average six-year-old has a speaking vocabulary somewhat in excess of 2500 words and that his meaning (or listening) vocabulary may be as large as 17,000 basic words and 7000 derivatives. He will have learned to weave the words in his speaking vocabulary into all types of sentences—simple, compound, and complex—averaging in length about five words. So extensive a growth in language in the preschool years reflects the wealth of concepts, interests, verbal skills, and thought-power that the teacher of young children can tap and utilize as she guides them along the road to reasonable efficiency in listening, speaking, reading, and writing.

The foregoing statements have been in terms of averages. Some children will have acquired only a limited vocabulary and be less facile than others in the use of sentences and less articulate. On the other hand, there will be children who are much more advanced than the average because of influences favorable to language growth. Among such influences are (*a*) high intelligence, (*b*) emotional stability based on a feeling of being wanted and loved at home, (*c*) being an only child who has associated with adults and thus has patterned his language after theirs, (*d*) being a girl, since boys develop more slowly than girls do, and (*e*) the normal environment of an upper middle-class home in which the parents use literate language, talk freely with their children about everyday activities, and also provide many enriching experiences such as travel and listening to stories. Retardation in language growth, then, may be due to (*a*) unusually low intelligence, (*b*) being shy or reticent because of feeling inadequate or unwanted, (*c*) being a twin or triplet, (*d*) being a boy and therefore probably slower to develop, or (*e*) coming from a home in which experiences are barren and the language patterns of adults are illiterate in type.

While the teacher is engaged with a reading group, the free-time activities shown in the frontispiece facing the opening of this chapter may be going on. They include imaginative art work with clay and paints or crayons; performance of classroom duties; dramatic play; writing a letter and mailing it at the classroom post office.

Teachers must, of course, accept each child as he is and carry him forward by providing appropriate experiences and activities so that the gifted child will not be held back and the retarded child can succeed at the level of his own possibilities.

Such are the facts that explain the degree and quality of language achievement that each child brings to school. Even more important is the nature of the child himself. What is the child in a first or second grade like?

Social Development   Unless the first-grade child has attended kindergarten, he will be accustomed to associating with his family and with neighbors, most of whom are older or younger than he. Entering the first grade may be a very strange experience indeed if, for the first time, the child is one of thirty children of about the same age and size. He may feel lost in the crowd, especially if he finds none of his customary playmates there. The teacher's first responsibility is to help him feel at home, to give him a feeling of personal identity even though he is, at the same time, learning to subordinate any personal wishes that do not coincide with those of the group. Learning to take turns, to share, to co-operate, to contribute for the benefit of others—such are the social learnings to be attained.

What characteristics must the teacher consider as she promotes the child's social learnings and development? In the first place, all young children are interested in the *here* and the *now*. The small child wants something this minute, this morning, today—not a half hour or a half day later. To him, tomorrow may never come, and yesterday is not important. He knows his home, his street, his shopping center, his classroom, and the playground; and it is with these places that the five- or six-year-old is mainly concerned. As he progresses into the seven- and eight-year stage, the child discovers an expanding environment and a lengthening time span. His learning activities can involve his larger community and its helpers who make his life safe and comfortable; he can plan more and more suitably for the morrow and for next week. He remembers better the lessons that yesterday brought in terms of group living and behavior.

Another characteristic common to the young child is egocentrism. With him it is the *big I* and the *little you*. This is a nature-ordained characteristic, but one susceptible to change through wise training and normal group experiences. The young child can and does learn to take turns and to share, to co-operate in group activities—especially those in which only a few children are involved in some joint enterprise—and to be considerate of others. He develops these characteristics and attitudes, not so much through being corrected and lectured to, as through living and doing. The young child must have firsthand experience if he is to develop social insight and acquire desirable attitudes and habits of social conduct.

The egocentrism of the young child is often reflected in his language. When a companion makes a statement such as "My puppy has learned to sit up," the child's response is usually not a question or remark about his companion's pet, but rather some remark about his own pet of which he has been reminded. He is likely to say, "My puppy learned that a long time ago," rather than "Your puppy must be smart," or "How did you teach him a trick like that?" However, the conversation and discussion of first- and second-grade children tend to outgrow mere parallelism, and to develop toward a meeting of minds. Such development will result if the school promotes situations in which pairs or small groups of children work and play together in enterprises directed toward a common goal, such as setting up a store or building a bookcase from crates or planning a dramatization.

Intellectual Characteristics The young child is generally a curious, active learner. There is much in the real world that is strange and marvelous, much that he does not understand, so many questions that he feels impelled to ask. He wants to feel and to touch, to taste and to smell, and to inspect closely. Sensory learning through manipulative activities is important in that it develops the child's awareness of the interrelationship of ideas and of sequential order; which, in turn, result in enrichment of vocabulary and increased power of expression.

Because his environment does contain so many puzzling wonders, the young child prefers the real to the make-believe. The world of fairies, elves, giants, and dragons belongs more to the child in the third and fourth grades who knows enough about reality to be able to distinguish between the factual and the fantastic. Again, these statements are made in terms of the average child. Some five-year-olds may be so advanced as to resemble the average seven-year-old; others may more nearly approach the characteristics of a child of four. However, with all children there is a sequence of development that progresses from the real things of the *here* and *now* to the realities of tomorrow or yesterday; then to those of long ago or a distant future; and eventually to an interest in the fanciful creatures and fictional episodes of literature and historical legend.

The beginner in school has a short attention span, and he is highly imitative. To take account of the former characteristic, the teacher will change activities frequently, keeping each one brief. Gradually, as maturation develops a lengthening span, the teacher adjusts the program by developing new interests that make it easy for the child to pay attention; by providing much physical activity; by appealing to the senses with colorful pictures and objects; and by using materials that children can manipulate. She also capitalizes on the child's natural imitativeness by using a well-modulated and pleasing voice, by enunciating clearly, and by stressing the correct forms of words in her speech, in her storytelling, and in informal oral reading activities. She is courteous, neat, poised, kindly; and her spirit and manner are sure to be reflected in the behavior of her pupils.

The first-grade child tends to be somewhat impetuous and noncritical in his learning activities. He draws his picture or writes his story, and then assumes the attitude of "I've done my job. What next?" On the other hand, the child in the second grade is past the early, crude stages of learning, and he is usually more self-critical. In fact, he is sometimes said to be in the "eraser age" because he uses his eraser more than either his pencil or his crayon as he writes and draws. Whatever he is learning to do, he wants to do it well.

Physical Development   The child in the early primary grades is an active, restless learner. The physiological demands of his growing body make it imperative that he not sit still too long, that he be permitted to move about in the process of learning. In reading, he is asked to go to the chart to "frame" a given word, or to dramatize a meaning. In social studies units, he constructs paints, or engages in dramatic play. He learns number relationships and facts through manual and verbal activity.

Though the child has rather good control of the larger muscles of his body, he still lacks co-ordination and control of the smaller muscles of his hands, feet, and eyes. The current practice of using manuscript writing instead of cursive writing in first and second grades is based on the fact that the former is less demanding on the smaller muscles than is cursive writing. In the early primary grades the child is still in the process of gaining control of his vocal organs and may be unable to sound certain parts of words; for example, *l, r, s, z, sh, th, br,* and *wh* sounds may not be mastered by some children until the age of seven or eight.

Social Environment as a Factor

When planning the language arts program, it is important that the teacher consider not only the language learnings that are desirable for the children in her charge, but also the social environment that is shaping their personalities and their expressional level. The cultural status of home and community, as well as trends and demands of the nation and the world at large, are strong formative influences. They also constitute the environment into which the children must fit. The school must plan a curriculum that will help each child to become a worthy, well-adjusted member of the society into which he is born.

Cultural Background At the beginning of Grade One, most of the *ideas* that children have to communicate will have come from preschool experiences. Within the family circle, children have overheard and engaged in conversation or discussion; listened to stories read aloud or told; received explanations and instructions; and shared letters to various members of the family. In addition, participation in various activities of the family and of the community will have contributed to the fund of ideas about which the children will talk. As the school year progresses, these out-of-school experiences will be augmented by both actual and vicarious experiences set up in the school program.

A second factor that influences the language program is the pattern of *speech habits* that children have developed before entering school. Some children will enunciate clearly and will habitually use correct speech forms. Those who enunciate poorly and who have developed habits of incorrect usage and pronunciation must be helped to more satisfactory levels of speech. Children who enter school with a good vocabulary have a great advantage; those with a meager fund of words are at a serious disadvantage, and they will need many and varied school experiences that will increase their fund of knowledge and of ideas and enrich their vocabulary.

Another aspect of the children's background that needs consideration is their *social development*. Have they learned to get along with other children? Are they willing to take turns? Do they sometimes assume leadership, and at other times follow willingly the leadership of others? Do they know and practice the common courtesies that children should observe? Are they too aggressive, or too timid and reserved? Have they learned to pay close attention when directions are being given or when classmates are telling of their experiences? Such social characteristics must be considered when the children's background is being studied.

Home relationships are a primary factor in establishing a child's emotional stability. As parents reveal their interest in the interests and activities of their children, the children feel that they have a definite place in the first social group of which they are a part—the family.

The School Environment The school is a part of the society into which the American child is born. Thus the school has a responsibility for setting up a democratic situation in which teacher and children plan together, work together, and evaluate together. In so doing, language becomes vital communication. The egocentric young child must learn to share; to take his turn both at play and at work; to subordinate his own wishes to group interests and decisions, yet at times to voice his desires in an effort to improve procedures and to bring about wiser decisions by the group when there seem to be sound reasons for doing so.

It is only as the child *lives* democratically that he will understand and adopt democratic ways. The language curriculum of the school must be actively and positively based on the democratic ideal for which our country stands in the world of today. The language arts program, therefore, must have a social setting in which genuine communication takes place. The curriculum cannot be a mere routine of practice exercises on correct usage, pronunciation, and the mechanics of written expression.

Emotional Atmosphere The child of today lives in an anxious world in which no one knows what the morrow will bring. The child is sure to hear of the perils of dictatorship, the dangers of atomic attack, the excessive cost of armament, and the like. While these specific concepts may not in themselves make the child anxious, it is the tensions and fears of adults as they read the newspapers, listen to the radio, watch television, and discuss the world problems that undeniably affect the child.

More directly the child is influenced by the problems that his family meets in trying to stretch the budget to care for the high cost of living. The food he eats, the clothes he wears, the apartment or house in which he lives, may be topics of concern in the mealtime conversations. Moreover, the family may be one of

Another instance in which children co-operate with parents in an enjoyable family activity. Participation and sharing in the home make it easier for the child to adapt himself to a group sharing in the schoolroom.

many who have recently moved out into the suburbs or into another state, and the child may suddenly have been uprooted and thus called upon to adjust himself to a new environment.

An unsettled home, an unsettled world, may well build tensions within a child. These tensions will be evidenced in school. At this point the language arts program can provide a great service as the child is given an opportunity to identify himself with

a child-character in a fine story of literary quality; to dramatize
a story where situations like his own are solved; to draw or write
as a release of his pent-up emotions. It is important, then, that
the language arts curriculum stress creative activity that provides
a release. Stability may well be promoted in such release.

Nature of the Modern Curriculum

The modern school curriculum should be planned in consideration of the findings of child study and of the social, national,
and international conditions of the time. Learnings should be
provided in terms of the child's own degree of maturation—of
what he is *now* interested in, and of what he is able to do *at his
current stage* of development. Since the child is an active learner,
the program should provide that he be helped to learn through
firsthand experience. Moreover, it should help him to face whatever social situations confront him, and guide him to a realistic
solution. The modern curriculum, then, is an activity program that
is socially centered; it is one in which children's language—
whether it be listening, speaking, reading, or writing—is integrated with all their learning activities.

The Place of Language in the Curriculum   There are usually
about 300 minutes in the school day. How many of these minutes involve language? Much of the time, someone will be talking while others listen and perhaps respond. A smaller portion
of the time will be devoted to writing. Even when there is not
actual communication of ideas among the members of the group,
there is likely to be activity that yields both ideas and vocabulary. Whether it be the period for social studies, for science,
or for reading instruction, there is almost continuous demand for
the enrichment and use of language expression.

Analysis of the two daily programs that follow will reveal how listening, speaking, reading, or writing will constantly be demanded in order to carry on the learnings of the entire school day. Note the blocks of time devoted to social studies activities and to reading. It is possible for the teacher to work with reading groups, using content and procedures determined on the basis of current needs and interests; or to distribute her time among individual children and short-term groups while the remainder of the class engages in independent activities. The programs were submitted by expert primary teachers, one favoring social studies activities early in the day and the other starting with reading.

DAILY PROGRAM A

Before school	Individual interests
9:00- 9:20	Entire group activities: checking attendance, sharing news, miscellaneous routine matters
9:20-10:15	Social studies block (*time allotment flexible*)

Planning activities	15 minutes
Learning activities	25 minutes
Evaluation; sharing; clean-up	15 minutes

10:15-10.30	Language activities (oral) related to the social studies (poems, stories, dramatization)
10:30-10:55	Play and rest period
10:55-11:20	Reading: Group 1 (*Seatwork and creative art*
11:20-11:45	Reading: Group 2 *for non-reading groups*)

* * * * * * *

12:45- 1:00	Story time
1:00- 1:25	Reading: Group 3 (*Seatwork and art for others*)
1:25- 1:45	Writing: Copying a dictated announcement or note; creative stories dictated to teacher and later read from a chart; practice on manuscript writing
1:45- 2:00	Rest or play
2:00- 2:20	Number activities
2:20- 2:40	Music

Before school   Free period for individually chosen activities
9:00- 9:20   Show-and-tell period; routine matters
9:20-10:35   Language arts block: Reading (*directed and free; individualized or by groups as situation demands*)
10:35-10:55   Play and rest period
10:55-11:55   Social studies block (*flexible time allotment to planning, learning activities, sharing and evaluation, and clean-up*)

                        ❋ ❋ ❋ ❋ ❋ ❋ ❋

1:00- 1:50   Language arts block
                Story time   15 minutes
                Language   35 minutes
                (*Original and reproduced stories growing out of story hour; dramatization; poems; writing, including dictation to teacher with occasional copying; practice on manuscript writing*)
1:50- 2:05   Rest or play
2:05- 2:20   Number activities
2:20- 2:40   Music

(NOTE: Art included as integral part of block activities)

Relationships among the Language Arts   Reading and language instruction are closely related, since the printed page can be interpreted only on the basis of the ideas and the vocabulary that are already a part of a child's language. Granted that the printed page does yield a new fact, a modified concept, or an unfamiliar word, each of these will have meaning only as it is interpreted in terms of the already familiar and well understood.

Words are a common denominator among the language arts. The child thinks in *words;* he expresses his ideas in *words;* he adds to his vicarious experiences by listening to or reading *words.* They are his vehicle of thought, of expression, and of impression. Therefore, any measures that will improve vocabulary in one of the language arts are likely to carry over into increasing or refining vocabulary in the other language arts. For example, young Ricky noted the word *resent* that had been used in a television program that he had enjoyed; and, later, when his father punished the puppy, Ricky exclaimed, "Daddy, I resent that!" In his future reading and in his writing of stories, Ricky would have no difficulty in meeting or using *resent* again.

Auditory discrimination is another characteristic that affects each of the language arts. Until a child hears a word correctly, he will not speak it correctly. For example, a young child called asparagus "sparrow grass" because she had heard and interpreted the word that way. Auditory and visual discrimination enter into word analysis in attacking new words in reading. Since the skills of word recognition and analysis are practically identical with the skills for learning to spell a word, auditory and visual discrimination are also important in spelling. Listening, speaking, reading, writing—auditory and visual discrimination underlie effectiveness in each of these four phases of the language arts.

Relation to Other Curriculum Areas   Activities and lessons in the social studies field or in science have a dual role in promoting language instruction. The children's background is being enriched as they acquire new concepts and new vocabulary. In addition, the periods devoted to these content areas afford many opportunities for the children to communicate. They discuss plans and later report on their progress in carrying out their plans; they dramatize or tell stories; they give and take instructions; they make explanations; or they assist in listing duties, the names of committee members, and materials needed for carrying on an activity. There may also arise, within a social studies or science activity, a situation that calls for the planning, writing, and mailing of a letter.

In addition, social studies learnings may stimulate spontaneous expression during free conversation or free writing periods. The following conversation illustrates typical pupil reactions after a trip to the farm.

TERRY. What a good time we had at the farm yesterday!

MISS BOND. I'm glad you enjoyed the visit, Terry. Would all of you like to tell what you enjoyed most?

MAE. I liked the little chicks best. Two of them ate cornmeal from my hand.

PATTY. One of the chicks let me hold it. It was so soft and downy. I held my other hand over its back, and the chick went to sleep.

Clifton   Quick   Gr. 2

Riddles

It is yellow.
It is made from milk.
It is put on bread.
What is it?
It is butter.

An original riddle, with content drawn from a group activity in social studies. The language value is apparent.

JACK. I liked the baby ducks. Do you remember how they quacked and came running to us? They like children, I suppose.

BOBBY. Oh! They just wanted something to eat. I gave them some of my sugar pops, and they certainly did like them.

KENNY. How funny the lambs were! I laughed and laughed when they kicked up their heels and ran all over the field. I wish I could have a little pet lamb to play with at home.

GUY. I think the baby pigs were the funniest of all. Did you see them stick their noses through the fence and wiggle them around? And what a queer noise they made when they ran off! "Woof, woof!" and off they ran. I shooed them three times just to hear them go "Woof!"

SALLY. I liked everything on the farm, but I think the kittens were best. Daddy's going to take me back to the farm next Sunday afternoon. Mr. Black told me that he would give me a kitten.

Additional outcomes of the farm experiences were stories and even riddles that some children wrote.

On the other hand, language learnings make a contribution to the social studies. The children speak more distinctly and effectively; they acquire the ability to speak or write in complete, clear sentences; they gain practice in organizing their ideas. Skill in using language aids other subjects.

Major Aspects of the Language Program

Group Expressional Activities At one period in the day, the girls and boys may relate personal experiences or observations in response to suggestions or questions from the teacher, who is seeking to develop a background for a story that is to be read. After the reading, the group may talk over episodes and characters in the story. At another period, they may discuss plans for an activity in the social studies program, such as setting up a classroom store patterned after the market or toy shop visited the day before, or writing a story summarizing their experiences on the trip. Other similar language situations rise throughout the day. The point is this: the speech and writing of first- and second-grade children in connection with any subject of the curriculum are to be recognized as a part of the language program. When the group engage in oral discussion or in co-operative writing, it is desirable for them to be seated in chairs arranged in a semicircle or in even more informal grouping such as clustering on a rug. However, even in an overcrowded, old-fashioned classroom with stationary seats, the spirit of free social communication can readily be developed through careful planning and guidance by the teacher.

Incidental Expression In addition to such periods as are described above, the language program includes the spontaneous speech of the girls and boys as they busy themselves with construction and crafts work. In fact, there is no more valuable kind of language than the informal communication of children as they work in small groups on such enterprises as painting, modeling, the making of a movie film, or the preparation of scenery for a dramatization. In such completely informal situations, children make their most effective social adjustment as they develop a feeling of the togetherness of the group that makes them conscious of common interests and that inspires even the timid child to communicate his ideas, raise questions, and offer suggestions.

Furthermore, such situations provide the opportunity for the teacher to survey the speech habits of individuals and of the group, and to determine those language needs that are to be met later by a program of definite instruction to meet those needs. It is to be kept in mind that the major function of the teacher's planned language instruction is *to improve children's natural and*

The Farm

Animals live on a farm.
They have homes.
They have families.
on the farm.
Farm animals are our
friends.

After a first-grade group had visited a farm, they talked over their experiences. Then they dictated a story of a predominant interest in their trip—the farm animals. The teacher, acting as secretary, wrote each sentence on the board, and the children read their own story. At a later period—perhaps the next day—they copied their story from the board.

spontaneous language. All children need a richer store of words to express ever-widening experiences; some may need to improve voice quality, enunciation, or articulation; some, to develop a better command of the sentence or perception of the sequence of ideas; some, to correct errors in usage; and others to improve their social adjustment. The instructional program in language must be planned, organized, and executed to meet such needs.

The teacher of language must be as much concerned with *what* children say as with *how* they say it—that is, with *im*pression (intake of ideas) as well as with *ex*pression (outgo). The language program must therefore be directed toward two major objectives: (*a*) the enrichment of children's experiences, or provision for the *content* of expression; and (*b*) guidance and instruction designed to improve the *manner* and *form* of expression.

Provision for Enrichment   A humorous picture post card shows a man seated on a globe, despairingly exclaiming, "Nothing on earth to write about!" Many a child inwardly echoes this remark when given the opportunity to talk or write during the language period.

A major responsibility of the teacher of an early primary grade is to provide enriching experiences for her group so that they may acquire a constantly growing "mental bank account" of ideas that will function both as an *impetus to expression* and as the *content of expression.* There are many means for providing such experiences. A story or poem that vividly portrays an event or an experience may be told or read to the children. By skillful questioning, the teacher can then lead the group to discuss what they have heard, and also to relate some personal experiences similar to the one presented in the story or poem. A picture, a filmstrip, or a motion picture will also awaken in the minds of the children various ideas that may serve as content for interesting discussion,

Co-operation between home and school is highly desirable. Here a parent has come into the classroom to sing ballads to a first-grade group. The attitude of parents to the school and to its interests and problems has strong influence on the children's attitude.

conversation, or stories. Trips to local points of interest will provide firsthand experiences in connection with social studies or science. On the other hand, children may be inspired to talk about their experiences outside school: for example, television programs they have enjoyed; books that have been read to them or that they may have read; simple tasks and pleasures in the home; objects they have made; games or play that they enjoy.

Social situations must also be provided in the classroom to offer opportunities for the development of the courtesies, or social language. The expected arrival of a visitor may provide a motivation for developing correct form for greetings and good-bys. A class party may stimulate interest in learning courteous expression in extending greetings, passing and accepting refreshments, playing games, and the like. In all such experiences, new ideas as to social relationship and responsibility are engendered, and new vocabulary and modes of expression attend upon those ideas.

It is not enough merely to provide children with opportunities to enrich their experience through active, participatory enterprises. They must also become keener and more discriminating in their observation. For example, they should be encouraged to watch quietly while a spider spins its web and snares its first victim; to look at some unfamiliar bird closely so that they can describe it; or to observe how a workman uses hammer and nails in order that they themselves may be able to develop better techniques of handling tools safely. It is necessary, then, not only to provide girls and boys with enriching experiences, but also to develop in them the ability to observe closely various objects, activities, and procedures in their environment.

Oral and Written Expression   Children need to talk over their observations and experiences since impressions are strengthened when they find expression in words. The attempt to explain, to describe, or to discuss an experience will, moreover, reveal haziness and gaps in information that point out the need for close observation to obtain additional information. Therefore the *intake* of ideas should always be accompanied with a correlative *outgo*, often in words, but sometimes in drawing, modeling, dramatization, or construction.

Most of the expression in the first and second grades should be oral, partly because the children have not yet mastered the mechanics of written communication (spelling, capitalization, and punctuation), but more largely because occasions for oral expression arise more frequently in real life than do occasions for writing.

The content of oral expression is, of course, of major importance. Yet distinct and accurate articulation and enunciation,

An impelling interest in books and their story content should be developed in children even before they learn to read. The knowing teacher will acquaint the children with the joys of reading by reading to them daily from juvenile books of high interest and with attractive illustrations. An added value is the enrichment of vocabulary as the stories are discussed or retold.

simple and clear-cut sentence structure, freedom from crude and illiterate misuse of words, a growing vocabulary, the ability to narrow a topic and to stick to the point—these, too, are objectives to be sought in the children's oral communication.

Until the latter half of the second grade, many children do not have sufficient command of the tools of writing to write for themselves. The teacher must then act as secretary to the individual or to the group and write down the ideas that are expressed. Often a group story or a group report that she has written on the board will be used as a reading chart. In some instances the girls and boys will want copies of their own to carry home, to mail, or to use in a booklet. Then they may copy what the teacher has written for them. It is important to encourage the children to hold to high standards for such copy work—not too difficult a task when their purpose for copying is important to them. Almost surely they will work for neat papers and accurate copying of spelling, punctuation, and capitalization.

Later they will be able to take exercises from dictation and also to complete an unfinished story, both processes serving as steps on the road to independent writing.

Objectives of Language Instruction

In setting up a language program that will provide for both impression and expression (intake and outgo), the first- or second-grade teacher must plan with definite objectives in mind. These objectives may vary, both as to nature and emphasis, from one locality to another, and some of them may not be fully met until near the end of the second grade. However, certain of them are constant in all situations, and the program of language can be pursued with all of them in mind. These objectives are listed under six categories on the following pages.

Objectives for first and second grades are very similar in nature, the program in the second grade being directed toward an extension and refinement of those interests and skills that are important in the first grade. Growth in the power of expression is continuous. As stated earlier in this chapter, some of the abler first-grade children will be far ahead of the slow-learning and low-average children in second grade. Only in connection with written communication are new skills introduced in the second grade.

I. To enrich the content of oral and written communication
   A. Through firsthand experiences, such as:
      Making soap or butter as pioneers did
      Taking trips and excursions for definite purposes
      Collecting specimens
      Setting up and labeling an exhibit
      Entertaining guests
      Having a birthday party
      Caring for pets, flowers, or germinating seeds
   B. Through language experiences, such as:
      Sharing news
      Participating in a show-and-tell period
      Planning daily activities and evaluating them
      Listening to stories, poems, explanations, and directions
      Using new words acquired through enriching experiences
      Dramatic play and dramatization
      Planning an assembly or party
      Acting as announcer or host
   C. Through a stimulating classroom environment that includes:
      A book corner with book shelves and a reading table
      A science center in which a museum can be developed
      A bulletin board for the display of pictures, notices, book lists, children's written stories of special interest
      Pictures featuring current centers of interest
      Films, filmstrips, and recordings
      Supplies to stimulate creative work, including crayons, paints, easels, clay, and simple tools

II. To build desirable attitudes toward listening
   A. **By fostering group relationships,** including:
      Group rapport that results in ease and confidence
      Co-operative spirit in group enterprises
      Willingness to share ideas and materials
      Sense of responsibility for contributing ideas and effort
   B. **Through provision for successful language experiences,** as in:
      Commanding interest of group through having something special and uniquely one's own to tell
      Learning new words that help to make ideas clear
      Learning new skills, such as letter form and spelling, as soon as readiness to learn is apparent (but not before)

III. To develop powers basic to expression
   A. **Through teacher guidance and questioning,** directed toward:
      Assimilation and organization of ideas and facts
      Relating new ideas to old ideas
      Comparison and contrast of observed data
      Adherence to topic under consideration
   B. **Through development, under the teacher's guidance,** of:
      Habits of attentive listening
      A sense of sequential organization
      Ability to stick to the point in discussion, group stories, and reports
      A sense of fitness of the form of expression for various types of written communication, such as labels, announcements, captions for pictures, blank-filling, signs, and lists
      A sense of need for each preceding type of communication
      A feeling for the importance of using correct forms in writing
      A sense of need for using clear and correct speech
   C. **By encouraging the creative tendencies,** in such forms as:
      Original stories, verse, plays

IV. To build socially acceptable habits
   A. **Through observation of correct practices**
   B. **Through development in social situations,** of:
      Habits of courtesy, attentiveness, and responsibility
      Use of accepted forms of greetings and thanks
      The art of give-and-take in conversation and discussion

Readiness to accept suggestions and helpful criticism by teacher and classmates

V. To develop desirable speech skills, such as:

A natural and pleasing voice

Distinct enunciation and correct pronunciation

A natural, easy manner and posture before a group

Avoidance of the run-on sentence (overuse of *and, so,* and *then*)

Elimination of immature speech habits, such as lisping

Substitution of correct language forms for illiterate ones

VI. To learn and to improve writing skills (largely for second grade)

A. Through observation of the teacher when writing

B. Through active participation in writing activities, to develop the following:

Neat daily written work arranged in correct form

Neat and accurate copying of announcements and letters (for the slower learners)

Writing co-operative stories and reports from the teacher's dictation, as a step toward independent writing

Correct spelling of more common words frequently used

Habitual correct use of capital letters and punctuation for such forms of written communication as the group employs

Habit of checking one's own written work before handing it in

Evaluation by Teacher and by Child

In a complete and wisely-conceived language program, evaluation is an essential feature. Both the teacher and the children should realize whether or not progress is being made toward the accomplishment of the objectives that have been set up. By studying models and comparing their own language products with such models, by setting up standards, by filing representative samples of work and comparing a recent composition with one written some time ago, and by other means consistent with the nature and purpose of communication, it is possible for the child to make a helpful evaluation of his progress toward the language goals of first and second grades.

A second-grade group planned to visit the library during the regular story hour in the juvenile room. Before going, they discussed standards of conduct for the trip. Then they listed questions to be used by each child in evaluating his conduct after returning from the trip. Their teacher wrote the questions on a chart; and, after returning from the trip, a period was provided for group and individual evaluation. Here is their evaluation chart:

How Well Did I Do?

On the way
1   Did I walk quietly?
2   Did I keep with the group?
3   Did I talk very quietly?

In the library
1   Did I listen well?
2   Did I thank Miss Wood?

In the first grade and with immature children in the second grade, it is essential for the teacher to assume much of the responsibility for evaluation. She must remember to be constructive at all times; to praise creditable achievements of every child, dull or bright, so that a feeling of self-confidence may eventuate; to offer helpful comments that will show each child how and where to improve. Never should she find fault; always she should encourage, direct, guide. To the greatest possible extent, she should develop abilities of self-appraisal in the child. Independence in evaluating his own work is a long-range goal for the child in the elementary school.

Most teachers find that making a check list of the accomplishments that are her language goals is a most helpful evaluative device. This check list may be placed on a large chart or on the pages of a loose-leaf notebook. Place the names of pupils at the head of columns; the goals may be listed down the left side of the chart or page. Thus the teacher can check off a point on which an individual pupil is progressing by placing a *plus sign* in the proper square; by putting a *minus sign* to indicate where the pupil needs help; by using a *star* to show unusual proficiency or growth; and a *capital N* to indicate that an explanatory note has been placed in the child's individual record folder to record data and facts that explain the child's problems.

The following chart was devised by one teacher as a means of checking and recording the progress of individual pupils:

Personal Development

A. Is physically equipped for learning to—
1 Listen well (good hearing)
2 See well (good eyesight)
3 Talk well (normal vocal organs)
4 Write reasonably well (motor co-ordination)
5 Participate in general (nutrition, sleep, physical defects)

B. Socially, is learning to—
1 Take his turn in group conversation, games, and the like
2 Share with others in work or play
3 Play and work harmoniously with others
4 Assume responsibility
5 Work independently
6 Follow directions
7 Be a leader in at least one type of activity

C. Is emotionally stable, and not—
1 Too shy or withdrawn
2 Too aggressive
3 Subject to temper tantrums

    4 Subject to fits of depression
    5 Moody
    6 Resistant

D. Intellectually, is—
    1 A slow, average, or quick learner
    2 Narrow, average, or rich in experiential background
    3 Particularly interested in __?__
    4 Lacking in __?__ types of experience
    5 Observant and curious, or disinterested and phlegmatic
    6 Resourceful, imaginative and creative; or matter-of-fact

Language Development

A. Listening:
    1 Has a short, average, or long span of attention
    2 Is developing a longer span
    3 Understands explanation and directions
    4 Follows directions well
    5 Enjoys hearing stories and poems
    6 Gains information through listening
    7 Follows the sequence of ideas
    8 Is a courteous listener when others speak

B. Speaking:
    1 Enunciates well
    2 Has trouble in sounding certain letters
    3 Pronounces words correctly
    4 Has a distinct, pleasing voice
    5 Is easy and poised in manner
    6 Sets off each sentence by itself
    7 Has a varied and growing vocabulary
    8 Uses vivid and interesting words
    9 Arranges ideas in good order
  10 Sticks to the point in group conversation or discussion
  11 Talks in parallel fashion, or can give and take in discussion
  12 Is willing to participate in oral language activities
  13 Is fluent and graphic in oral expression

14 Is original and creative
15 Is habitually correct in use of words
C. Writing:
1 Is neat in all written work
2 Is careful in forming letters
3 Uses punctuation marks correctly
4 Uses capital letters correctly
5 Is observant of correct spelling
6 Is careful to use complete sentences
7 Is observant of the sequence of ideas
8 Is interested in learning to write by himself
9 Is free and spontaneous in writing brief notes and stories

Bibliography

EQUIPMENT

Association for Childhood Education. *Recommended Equipment and Supplies* for Nursery, Kindergarten, Primary, and Intermediate Schools. (Pages 13-36 list equipment for a primary group of 25 children.) Washington 5, D. C.

INTAKE OF IDEAS

BEERY, ALTHEA. "Listening Activities in the Elementary School," *Elementary English,* February, 1946

DAWSON, MILDRED A. "Making Friends of Books." Language Arts Notes, No. 4. World Book Company, Yonkers-on-Hudson, New York

FLEISCH, MARIAN. "Pictures Help Vocabulary Growth," *Elementary English,* December, 1945

STEPHENS, ADA D. *Providing Developmental Experiences for Young Children.* Practical Suggestions for Teaching, No. 11. Bureau of Publications, Teachers College, Columbia University, New York 27

WILT, MIRIAM. "What Is the Listening Ratio in Your Classroom?" *Elementary English,* May, 1949

COMMUNICATION OF IDEAS

APPLEGATE, MAUREE. *Helping Children Write.* International Textbook Company, Scranton 9, Pennsylvania

Bureau of Reference, Research, and Statistics, New York City. *Developing Children's Power of Self-Expression through Writing.* Board of Education, New York

BURROWS, ALVINA T., and Others. *They All Want to Write.* Prentice-Hall, Inc., Englewood Cliffs, New Jersey

POOLEY, ROBERT. *Teaching English Usage.* Appleton-Century-Crofts, Inc., New York 1

GENERAL

BAKER, ZELMA W. *The Language Arts, the Child, and the Teacher.* Fearon Publishers, San Francisco

Cincinnati Public Schools. *New Primary Manual* and *New Intermediate Manual.* Curriculum Bulletins, Nos. 300 and 400

DAWSON, MILDRED A. *Guiding Language Learning.* World Book Company, Yonkers-on-Hudson, New York

Department of Public Instruction, State of Indiana. *A Good Start in School.* Curriculum Bulletin, No. 158

HERRICK, VIRGIL, and JACOBS, LELAND (editors). *Children and the Language Arts.* Prentice-Hall, Inc., Englewood Cliffs, New Jersey

JENKINS, FRANCES. *Language Development in Elementary Grades.* Thomas Nelson and Sons, New York 17

National Council of Teachers of English. *The English Language Arts* and *Language Arts for Today's Children.* Appleton-Century-Crofts, Inc., New York 1

National Society for the Study of Education. Forty-Third Yearbook, Part II. *Teaching Language in the Elementary School.* University of Chicago Press, Chicago 37

TIDYMAN, WILLARD, and BUTTERFIELD, MARGUERITE. *Teaching the Language Arts.* McGraw-Hill Book Company, Inc., New York 36

2 | *Experience: The Basis for Language Growth*

An important though widely ignored aspect of the program in language arts is provision for enriching experiences that will build up the requisite "mental bank account"—the store of ideas that will provide the content of expression. Children must have an abundance of real and vicarious experiences that will give them ideas and facts to talk and write about; and they must have an adequate vocabulary at their command in order to express these ideas clearly and accurately.

Most of the ideas in the minds of young children entering school have originated from out-of-school experiences, such as watching Mother and Father at work; helping with certain home tasks; running errands; questioning elders about anything and everything within the range of observation; playing with other children;

working in the garden; walking or riding through the country or town; watching television or motion pictures; looking at comic strips and listening as Father or Mother reads them aloud; looking at books and listening to stories read to them from books; shopping with Father or Mother; taking trips with parents.

Wide-open eyes and alert ears, a questioning mind, busy hands, and running feet, all help to build up a background of ideas and information that the teacher may call upon in developing the arts and skills of language expression.

A Program of Group Participation

As stated in the preceding chapter, the personality of the child —that is, his make-up in terms of attitudes, habits, emotions, and interests—has been pretty well established by the time he comes to school. Particularly is he likely to be self-centered and not much concerned with the welfare of others.

Learning through Sharing It is therefore the problem of the teacher in the first or second grade to set up situations that call for group endeavor. The naturally individualistic young child becomes a social and co-operative classroom citizen as he joins with the other children in carrying out an enterprise. He helps to make and keep the play corner orderly; he works with his classmates in building a play store; he helps to plan a trip to the fire station.

In all such enterprises, conditions should be such as to contribute to the child's emotional stability. If he is to have a sense of security, he should feel wanted. He should also be so directed that he will have a good chance of being successful. There should be some areas of activity in which he can exercise leadership; and, on the other hand, there should be occasions when he recognizes the advisability of following others.

In both Grade One and Grade Two, children vary as greatly in their emotional and social backgrounds as they do in their ideational ones. Some are well adjusted socially: that is, they are ready and willing to share with others, to take turns, to be either leaders or followers, to be considerate and courteous, to be responsible and prompt, and to fit in where they may serve the group needs. Others lack one or more of these characteristics because of the lack or the imbalance of earlier training. Some children are too retiring; some, over-confident and even aggressive; some are indifferent to the welfare and happiness of their associates, and generally maladjusted. All vary to some degree in their established interests, though primary children are generally interested in whatever is colorful, concrete, or actively in motion. However, some are more interested in animals and birds, others in policemen and firemen, others in airplanes—the character and type of previous experiences having been a determining factor.

Developing Learning Habits In the skills and habits that underlie learning, young children vary also. In general, their span of attention is short. The teacher will need to initiate each activity with such appeal as to arouse interest and attention from the beginning; and then to exercise sufficient insight to terminate the activity before interest lags. She should keep periods of learning brief, especially in the early first grade. She can help the children increase their attention span naturally by planning for manipulative activities, by providing for color and movement in the materials she handles, and by appealing directly to the senses.

Children generally need to have their powers of observation sharpened. Whenever an interesting object has been brought to the "show-and-tell period," the teacher should steer the children's observation by pointed questions or by comments that direct attention to important features. On a walk around the block or in a park, she may halt the group to notice a swallowtail butterfly flitting among the flowers in a garden, the oriole nest dangling from a twig, the flash colors of the robin flying across a lawn. In the classroom, she may make up riddles describing one of the children or an object in the classroom. In all sorts of ways, she will help the children to observe closely, to hear, to touch, and then to describe with increasingly keen discrimination.

Listening Activities

Though children learn much through their own observation and active participation, they also learn much through contact with their fellows. They profit from conversation periods in which classmates relate firsthand experiences, or reproduce stories and verse heard at home. New interests may be born, social attitudes improved, and concepts broadened as the children tell one another about their personal experiences. Thus it is that listening becomes so important a phase of the language curriculum.

In the sequential development of the four language arts, listening comes first as the baby hears the sounds about him and gradually learns to attach meaning to them. Thus listening lays the groundwork for subsequently learning to speak, to read, and to write. It is a determiner of a child's speech patterns—the words that make up his preschool vocabulary, his voice quality, his enunciation and pronunciation of words, his patterns for framing sentences. That is, the child listens to the speech of others and then imitates. This tendency to imitate persists after his entrance into school. Hence the teacher should maintain a desirable quality of voice and speech as a means of improving the oral expression of her pupils.

Listening is, in fact, as vital and significant a part of the language arts curriculum as are speaking and writing. It provides much of the *intake* so necessary to a rich and effective language program. Since there is listening whenever there is talking, occasions in which listening takes place occur throughout the school day. The teacher reads or tells stories; she shares poems with the children. Girls and boys volunteer to share their individual reading or the stories they have heard at home. Likewise there is much to be gained as children converse and discuss experiences in connection with their reading and other learning activities.

Recordings, Radio, Motion Pictures, and Television There are, in addition, some special kinds of listening in the modern primary school. For example, there are recorded poems and stories for children, and also recordings that give instructions for rhythms and for story plays to accompany music. Outside the school, radio, motion pictures, and television bring enriching opportunities for listening. There are weather reports and even some news items that children can understand. There are literary offerings such as storytelling and dramatizations of stories. Similar opportunities are increasingly provided at the school through the use of radio and record players in the classroom. The offerings of the community should be noted by the teacher so that she may become alert to such available radio, motion picture, and television programs as will be of value and interest to young children.

Training in Listening It is highly important that the teacher train children to be thoughtful listeners. If she establishes the practice of giving directions only once—plainly, clearly, impressively—the children soon realize that they are expected to know what to do after a single telling. Some occasions may call for repetition; but in general it should be the teacher's aim to give directions well the first time so that no pupil learns *not to listen* because he knows that they will be repeated.

As children listen to musical recordings, the rhythm has strong emotional appeal, and children respond to it physically. Similarly, when they listen to poems that appeal strongly to the senses, or to stories that have dramatic action, they tend to respond vocally or physically.

Training in listening is especially necessary in these modern times. Most homes have radios and television sets that are turned on much of the time, even when conversation and family discussions are going on. The child must necessarily learn to shut out either the family's talking or the program. He therefore is learning *not* to listen to one thing in order that he may listen to another. Children tend, for this reason, to be quite adept in tuning out what does not interest them; and the teacher needs to be sure that she herself is sufficiently interesting and compelling so that the children do not tune her out, even unintentionally.

Ways of Improving Listening The observant teacher knows that she can help children to listen with close and continued attention if she will provide for simultaneous visual appeal so that the eye reinforces the ear; she will associate listening with opportunities for the children to do things, to participate. That is, listening is aided when the teacher takes into account the children's tendencies and their natural interests in active and concrete types of learning.

Children may be helped to grow in listening power if the teacher follows some or all of the following suggestions:

1 Be sure that the children have a purpose for listening, a purpose that is suitable to their level of maturity, to the type of material, and to the occasion. A different mind set is called for as purposes vary. There may be *casual listening* for enjoyment, *intent listening* to ascertain the answer to a question, and *critical listening* to select the best of several stories.

2 Provide a classroom atmosphere conducive to listening: quiet, comfortable, relaxed. Arrange that the young listeners sit as close as possible to the speaker or oral reader.

3 Lead the children to expect meaning in whatever they are listening to. Encourage them to ask questions when they do not understand or when they want further details. Encourage an attitude of mental curiosity.

4 Always prepare the children for listening by recalling related familiar experiences or materials; by developing new words that are likely to be heard; and by questions that arouse curiosity or a feeling of mild suspense.

5 Remember that opportunities to listen for different purposes arise throughout the school day. Take advantage of them.

6 Provide that the pupils purposefully summarize or utilize what they have heard through such follow-up activities as dramatization, making an illustrative mural or individual pictures, constructing illustrative models, and the like.

7 Help the children to set up a growing list of standards for effective listening so that they will learn when they should listen, how they should listen, and what it is important to remember in specific instances.

Group Experiences Provided by the School

Rich Curricular Experiences   Naturally the school program should stress firsthand observation and participation in enriching activities. Into the classroom may be brought actual objects, such as a milkweed pod beginning to open and discharge its flyaway seeds; a budding branch; a brooding hen with a nestful of eggs; clusters of frogs' eggs that will produce lively tadpoles; a collection of bird pictures for a frieze; Indian relics; and many other real things. These may become the objects of directed daily observation, may occasion timely discussion or conversation, and provide content for group or individual stories or reports.

The children may sometimes be taken out to study the trees on the playground. They may take a trip to a nearby brook to observe plant and animal life, or walk around the city block to observe specific neighborhood activities. They may visit a local grocery store in order to make plans for a play store, or visit an airport or a dairy farm. Numerous possibilities for reaching out into the community to acquire new experiences and new ideas present themselves. Perhaps social studies, or science, or arithmetic will be the curricular center for certain of these activities. Even so, the language program benefits through the enrichment

The illustration at the opening of this chapter shows a group of children on a visit to a farm. For some days after the trip, the children's experiences there motivated conversation and discussion, in the course of which vocabulary was enriched and experiences in oral expression developed. Part of the discussion grew out of the planning for a model farm that the group wanted to set up; and the construction work entailed and the modelling of the animals in clay provided profitable contingent values.

of the children's ideas and vocabulary, improved social attitudes and conduct, the development of keener powers of observation, and growth in the power of selective thinking.

Many of the experiences itemized in the preceding paragraph suggest participation in an integrated curricular program, at least for part of the day. For example, when Indian relics have been brought in because of their contribution to a unit on Indian life, there will arise the need for an exhibit, entailing classification of objects, arrangement by types, and preparation of legends and labels; and invariably, in the progress of the enterprise, there is occasion for discussion of plans and reporting of data. Children learn not only through observation, but also through doing.

We had snow.
It is on cars.
It is on the trees.
It is on the
houses.

Darlene

Daily observation of weather as a feature of science study in a first grade led to a group report or story each morning. The children dictated the sentences that comprised the story and the teacher wrote them on the board. Later the children copied the report, and each child kept his report in a "Weather News" folder. Note the fairly good letter form and spacing for a child in mid first grade.

The modern school program affords many other occasions for talking and writing. Pupil helpers are selected to do various classroom chores, and plans for doing these chores properly are discussed. Lists of names of committee members are prepared and posted, and there are frequent occasions when the committees' work requires discussion and evaluation. Standards for conduct in the halls, on the stairs, and on the playground are discussed and posted. Each morning the children can participate in making special plans for the day.

Still other activities in the modern school afford occasions for communication. Training in courtesy is an essential in any classroom. Children discuss consideration for one another: taking turns, sharing toys and equipment, making the new girl or boy feel welcome, finding a place in the activities for any child who has a tendency to withdraw, and the like. The play period is a particularly fertile source of topics for discussion of such problems as planning for safety measures and for the kinds of play procedures that reflect good sportsmanship.

Stimulating Environment Bare walls, desks in straight rows, shelves offering only the required textbooks—these are not the earmarks of a schoolroom where children *live and learn*.

The modern schoolroom has an environment rich in opportunities for learning and in inducements to learn. There are library books on the shelves in a reading corner where the children may browse or seek definite information. There is a display of especially attractive books that the teacher will read to the children. A bulletin board affords an ever-changing variety of pictures, announcements, news accounts written by children, or lost-and-found advertisements. From day to day, the children or the teacher will bring in objects of interest to be put on exhibit and to be discussed at appropriate times. Almost always there are

*The "reading corner" or library corner is an important feature of
the primary classroom. Shelves offering attractive and interesting books that have appeal for six- to eight-year-olds provide both
a stimulant and an aid to an effective program of reading instruction. In addition, the story content of the books presents
both ideas and vocabulary to enrich language expression.*

living things: a pet or two, an aquarium or terrarium, and flower-
ing plants. Near the school there may be a nature trail with its
anthills, frog pond, wild flowers, and bird haunts. Stimulating
and rich, but never confusing, is the environment of the school
in which children are constantly broadening their background of
experience and developing wholesome attitudes and habits of
conduct. (See the first item of the *Bibliography* on page 31 for
additional suggestions.)

Vicarious Experiences It should be realized that the reading
program in itself is a source of language growth. In fact, the
reading program is a considerable part of the broader language
arts program. As children and teacher share favorite literary se-
lections, the girls and boys gain vicarious experiences. Always

there will be discussion preliminary to the reading of a new story, and the illustrations are studied and interpreted. The story is again discussed after the reading. Individual children often volunteer to tell similar stories that they have read, or to relate an experience suggested by incidents in the story. Frequently there is informal dramatization to enhance enjoyment of the story, reinforce comprehension, and heighten appreciation. Thus does reading instruction provide sources of topics for vital expression on the part of children. Simple picture books, filmstrips, recordings, and the available textbooks in the social studies, science, or health are equally fertile sources. Truly does the teacher of first and second grades teach language all day long.

An Experience Unit for Grade One

One spring morning Ray brought a downy yellow duckling to school. His Uncle Dan, who lived at Clover Farm, had given it to Ray. Naturally the children asked many questions about the duckling and about the farm where it was born, and a lively discussion opened the school day. The arrival of the duckling provided the following news story for the day, which the children dictated and the teacher recorded on the board.

Fluffy

Ray has a baby duck.
It came from his uncle's farm.
He brought it to school.
The baby duck is yellow.
It is soft and fluffy.
We call the baby duck Fluffy.

Miss Brown had hoped that some interest in farm life would arise during the spring season; for the time when the earth comes to life in grass and flowers and when animal babies are born is an appropriate time for the children to have an experience centered on farm life. In anticipation of such an occasion, she had been saving the farm stories in the various readers and in library books, and had planned to show filmstrips on baby animals.

In the wake of the new interest in farm animals that was aroused by the duckling, the children read many stories of life on the farm. They dramatized some of them, enjoyed the filmstrips, discussed the information given in them, drew pictures of aspects of farm life, learned songs relating to the farm.

As the children drew, Miss Brown wrote for each child the one- or two-sentence story about his picture that he dictated. The child copied the story as a legend for his picture.

Several of the children modeled farm animals. One boy suggested that the models be placed in the exhibit case in the main hall. This the class decided to do. One group of children prepared labels for the models. Putting up this display stimulated the idea that the group might like to prepare a complete farm exhibit for their fathers and mothers to see on Parents' Day.

"Could we take a trip to Clover Farm?" one alert boy asked. "I know that Daddy will take some of us in his car, if Ray's uncle will let us visit his farm."

The group enthusiastically took up this idea. Under Miss Brown's guidance, they talked over plans that would have to be made if a trip into the country were to be taken. As suggestions were made, Miss Brown wrote this list of questions on a chart:

1 How can we get permission from Ray's uncle ?
2 When may we go?
3 How many cars will be needed?
4 Whose father or mother will lend a car?
5 What do we want to see?
6 What questions do we want to ask?

Naturally, the children talked at home about the proposed trip, and some of the parents were persuaded to offer the use of a car. Ten cars were offered, provided that the trip was planned for a convenient day.

The next problem was how to get in touch with Ray's uncle. One of the children suggested a telephone call. Ray offered to make the request if Miss Brown would call the number. The group planned what Ray should say in making the request. Then Ray talked with his uncle and found out that the next Monday would be a convenient day for their trip.

It was found that seven cars would be available the next Monday. But the parents wanted to be sure of the plans, and they asked that some information be given them in writing. The group planned the following announcement, which the teacher wrote on the board at their dictation. All the children copied it, and the class selected seven neat papers to be sent to the parents.

> We will go to Clover Farm.
> We want to go at nine o'clock Monday.
> We will wait at the front door of the school.
> There will be four children in each car.
> We will start back at eleven o'clock.

On Monday, the seven cars were loaded and the children visited Clover Farm. Here they saw baby chicks, ducklings, frisky lambs, roly-poly pigs, two families of frolicsome kittens, and several mischievous puppies. Ray's Aunt Ellen allowed some of the children to help her feed the poultry. Uncle Dan let one boy feed an orphan lamb from a bottle. Everyone looked through the woven-wire fence at the pigs and lambs, where some babies were getting a warm meal from their mothers. Later the children were shown how to hold young kittens and puppies without hurting them, and were permitted to pet them.

*Observation and care of a family of chicks motivated interesting
activity in a classroom, including discussion of plans for their
care, dictated news items about the habits and growth of the
chicks, as well as drawing of pictures and the molding of models.*

The next morning, and indeed for days to follow, there were
facts and ideas for enthusiastic conversation and discussion. New
words were used, such as *woolly* lambs, *curly-tailed* pigs, *clucking*
hens, and the like.

During periods of free time, some girls and boys went to the
easels and painted farm scenes. Several of the pictures were so
good that the children expressed a desire to make a "movie" that
would picture their visit to Clover Farm. This suggestion led to

a discussion of what scenes to paint; which children should plan and arrange the scenes to paste on a long strip of wrapping paper; how large to paint the pictures. As plans were unfolded and decided upon, the teacher listed them on a chart.

At his desk, each child drew one or more farm scenes of his own choosing. As the children were drawing, the teacher moved among them. She wrote down the label or legend that each artist wished to attach to his picture, if chosen. Each day some pictures were held up and evaluated by the group, who then selected those to be pasted on the "film." A committee of four children was chosen to arrange the pictures in proper sequence. The teacher, with the aid of the committee, pasted the pictures on a long strip of paper and attached the labels or legends under each picture.

While some children had been painting pictures, others had modeled more farm animals from clay. Tom brought a toy barn from home, and some of the group made fences to mark off the various animal enclosures and meadows, such as those that surrounded the barn at Clover Farm. From this beginning, a complete layout of Clover Farm eventuated.

At appropriate times, Miss Brown asked questions to stimulate and guide the group in composing the story of their trip to the farm. At each period, one episode in the trip was discussed. The children composed sentences to tell the facts, and Miss Brown wrote them on a large chart. There were eleven stories in all, entitled as follows:

How We Went to Clover Farm	The Orchard
The Big Barn	Watching the Pigs
The Sheep and Lambs	The Horses and Colts
Feeding the Chickens	The Kittens
The Cows and Calves	The Puppies

The Big Tractor

Here is the first story composed by the children:

How We Went to Clover Farm

On Monday we went to Clover Farm.
Clover Farm belongs to Ray's uncle.
It is on Willow Road.
Seven mothers drove us in their cars.
We rode three miles.

The eleven charts were preserved and bound together as a book. For weeks the group enjoyed reading their book about Clover Farm. On Parents' Day the stories were read to the visitors, and several children gave brief reports on some of their experiences at the farm.

From one young duckling's visit to the school there had eventuated a rich experience that provided occasion for almost every variety of oral and written expression in which first-grade children engage.

Experiences in Grade Two

On the second-grade level, there may be experiences similar to the one outlined for Grade One. One such occasion may be an outgrowth of work in science, such as a walk through the woods, a park, or a garden, or along a hedgerow to observe seeds and seed pods.

Another major experience may concern the study of foods, such as a visit to a neighboring market, with the setting up of a play store or the making of a foods booklet as outcomes. Still others may be connected with the teaching of health and safety, or may concern class events, such as a birthday party or a parents' visiting day.

Countless opportunities do arise, for children's interests are many and varied. The alert teacher will recognize and seize each opportunity. Once an interest is set in motion, the resourceful teacher will see opportunities for (*a*) enrichment of experience that will awaken the children's minds to new facts and ideas; (*b*) expansion of meaningful vocabulary; (*c*) oral expression in the form of conversation or discussion, reporting or explaining, reading stories or poems, and dramatization; (*d*) different types of recorded expression, such as listed plans, questions, materials, or names; a group or individual news story; picture legends, or labels for exhibited objects; and group stories that recount experiences. In the course of such experiences, the technicalities of oral and written expression for which children in Grade Two have need may be taught with more assurance of permanent learning than can be guaranteed from didactic, separate teaching of isolated skills in which the children have no particular interest. Here are listed some units that have proved fruitful in many schools:

Grade I	*Grade II*
Living in My Home	People Who Help Us
Animals; Pets	Mapping Out Our Community
A Visit to the Farm	Summer Fun
Safety All Day	Let's Be Healthy
Holiday Fun	Bird Friends
Christmas and Toys	Stories to Play
Poems We Love	A Play Store

SUGGESTED LISTS OF UNITS

RESOURCE UNITS

Series published by the Quarrie Company and by World Book Encyclopedia, Chicago, Illinois

The Instructor Illustrated Series, F. A. Owen Publishing Co., Dansville, New York

ILLUSTRATIVE UNITS

Denver Public Schools. *A Program in English: A Guide for Teaching the Language Arts*, 1953

Grade I: The Circus, pages 9-13
Grade II: Summer Fun, pages 15-20
List of graded units, pages 197-198

State Department of Instruction, New Mexico: *Language Arts, Teachers Handbook, Grades 1 and 2*. Bulletin 18, 1953. Units with listed instructional materials, pages 54-103

SOURCES OF FILMSTRIPS

Here are given the addresses of the organizations that publish the filmstrips that are listed on pages 53-54. These addresses were correct as of the date of publication of this book, and the materials listed were available. However, commercial organizations do change their addresses on occasion; sometimes publications are discontinued; and often new publications are issued.

It is suggested, therefore, that the teacher who is interested in keeping abreast of the publication of films and filmstrips secure the latest catalogs from the publishers of such materials so that she may secure the newest and best materials on the market.

Before the name of each publisher listed, there is given the symbol that will identify the publisher of each filmstrip; for instance, EBF will indicate Encyclopaedia Britannica Films.

EBF   Encyclopaedia Britannica Films, Inc., 1150 Wilmette Avenue, Wilmette, Illinois

EGF   Eye Gate House, Inc., 27-16 41st Avenue, Long Island City 1, New York

ICPP   Informative Classroom Pictures Publishers, 31 Ottawa Avenue, Northwest, Grand Rapids 2, Michigan

JH   Jam Handy Organization, 2821 East Grand Boulevard, Detroit 11, Michigan

NFBC   National Film Board of Canada, 1270 Avenue of the Americas, New York 20

SVE Society for Visual Education, Inc., 1345 West Diversey Parkway, Chicago 14, Illinois

SF Stillfilm, Inc., 35 Raymond Avenue, Pasadena 1, California

VEC Visual Education Consultants, Inc., 2066 Helena Street, Madison 4, Wisconsin

YAF Young America Films, Inc., 18 East 41st Street, New York 17

SOURCES OF FILMS

Of the sources of filmstrips, two also provide films that are listed on page 55. These are EBF and YAF. Additional sources of films are listed below.

Cor. Coronet Films, 65 East South Water Street, Chicago 1, Illinois

FA Film Associates of California, 10521 Santa Maria Boulevard, Los Angeles 25

GP Gateway Productions, Inc., 1859 Powell Street, San Francisco 11

McG. H. McGraw-Hill Book Company, Text-Film Department, 330 West 42nd Street, New York 36

Ster. Sterling Films, 205 East 43rd Street, New York 17

WLF Wild Life Films, 5149-5151 Strohm Avenue, North Hollywood, California

SUGGESTED FILMSTRIPS

HOME AND SCHOOL

At Home and at School with Tom and Nancy (JH) (6 in set: Beginning the Day; Safely to School; Work at School; Lunchtime and Play; Birthday Party; Fun at Home)
We Go to School (YAF)

PETS

Care of the Cat (VEC)
Pet Stories (EBF) (6 in set: Goldfish, Kitten, Puppy, Parakeet, Rabbit, Turtle)
Our Pets (EGF) (9 in set: Dog, Rabbit, Cat, Chicken, Turtle, Horse, Canary, etc.)

FARM

Animals on the Farm (EGF)
Farmer's Animal Friends (JH) (6 in set: Cats, Chickens, Cows, Horses, Pigs, Sheep)
Baby Animals and Birds (on the Farm) (SF)

WILD LIFE

Animal Tracks (NFBC)
Animals and Their Ways (EGF) (9 in set: Babies, Pests, Insects, Care, Adjustment to Environment, Hardships, etc.)
Bird and Animal Babies (SVE)　　　Birds of Our Community (SVE)
Birds Grow (JH)　　　　　　　　　Homes of Birds (SVE)

CIRCUS AND ZOO

Circus Animals (VEC)　　　　　　Setting Up the Circus (VEC)
Circus Days (SF)　　　　　　　　Animals of the Zoo (SVE)

COMMUNITY HELPERS

Our City (ICPP)　　　　　　　　Our Police Department (EBF)
Our Fire Department (EBF)　　　　Our Post Office (EBF)
Community Helpers Series (YAF) (Set of 6: Bus Driver, Doctor, Fireman, Grocer, Mailman, Policeman)
Community Helpers (SVE) (Set of 5: Baker, Fireman, Grocer, Policeman, Postman)

SUGGESTED FILMS

HOME AND SCHOOL

On the Way to School (Cor.)
How Machines and Tools Help Us (Cor.)
City Pets: Fun and Responsibility (Cor.)

CITIZENSHIP

Let's Be Good Citizens at Home (GP)
Let's Be Good Citizens at School (GP)
Let's Be Good Citizens in Our Neighborhood (GP)
Let's Be Good Citizens in Our Town (GP) (Post Office, Police, Fireman)
Beginning Responsibility: Taking Care of Things (Cor.)

FARM

The Farmer (EBF)
Farm Babies and Their Mothers (FA)
How Animals Help Us (Cor.)

WILD LIFE

American Wild Life (WLF)
Animal Homes (EBF)
Animals of Our Storybooks (Cor.)
Birds of Our Storybooks (Cor.)
We Explore the Beach (Cor.)
Adventures of Willie Skunk (YAF)
Andy's Animal Alphabet (McG. H.)
Hoppy the Bunny (Cor.)
Let's Take a Walk along the Brook (GP)

CIRCUS AND ZOO

A Circus Wakes Up (Ster.)
Zoo Babies (Cor.)
Zoo Families (FA)

MISCELLANEOUS

Spring Is an Adventure (Cor.)
Calendar Days, Weeks, Months (Cor.)

COMMUNITY HELPERS

Discovering the Library (Cor.)
Stores in Our Community (Cor.)
Jimmy Visits the City (Cor.)
(Also see entries under "Citizenship" preceding.)

HOLIDAYS

Christmas Gift (EBF)
Halloween Party (EBF)
A Thanksgiving Play (EBF)
Special Days in February (Cor.)
Easter Surprise (EBF)
Littlest Angel (Cor.)

STORY

Monkey and the Organ Grinder (Cor.)
The Curious Cub (Ster.)
Toyland Escapades (Ster.)
Two Little Raccoons (YAF)

RECORDINGS

Audio Education, Inc., 55 Fifth Avenue, New York 3
"How Do You Talk?" Album ABC10 (speech skills)
Listen and Do Records, Volume III
   "Panda Balloon" and "Jocko, the Dancing Monkey"

Children's Record Guild, 27 Thompson Street, New York 13
   The Carrot Seed CRG 1003   Train to the Farm CRG 1011
   Grandfather's Farm CRG 5016   Train to the Zoo CRG 1001

Columbia Records, Inc., 799 Seventh Avenue, New York 36
   Cinderella MJ 32   Puss in Boots MJ 33
   Jack and the Beanstalk MJ 31   Peter Rabbit JL 8008

Decca Records, Inc., 50 West 57th Street, New York 19
   Manners Can Be Fun 90010

Educational Record Company, Charleston, Illinois
   Poetry Appreciation Series, Volume I

Radio Corporation of America, Camden, New Jersey
   Little Black Sambo WY 383
   The Little Engine That Could (by Paul Wing) WY 384
   Little Nipper, Fire Chief WY 2010
   Snow White and the Seven Dwarfs WY 33
   Winnie and Kanga Y 439
   Winnie-the-Pooh Y 438

Simmel-Meservey, Inc., Beverly Hills, California
   Tuneful Tales (by Martha Blair Fox)
      (1) The Laughing Jack-o'-Lantern
          The Nutcracker and King Mouse
          The White Easter Rabbit
      (2) The Shoemaker and the Elves
          The Little Engine That Could
          The Three Little Pigs
          Johnny Cake

Young People's Records, 100 Sixth Avenue, New York 13
   Building a City   Let's Play Zoo YPR 802
   Rainy Day   Out-of-Doors YPR 724
   The Little Cowboy   When I Grow Up YPR 725
   The Little Fireman   When the Sun Shines
   Little Indian Drum   Whoa! Little Horses, Lie Down

CHAPTER 3 | *Informal Oral*
Communication

Much of the oral communication of children in the early primary grades is completely spontaneous and unplanned. In the play corner, at the easel, during constructional activities, the children quietly chat and talk over their plans. Often they will play the story they have just read or heard, and do so with a minimum of planning. The educational values of such informal oral communication are high because it is through such spontaneous interchange of ideas that children grow socially and emotionally.

Exchange of News Items

In the first grade, it is common practice for the teacher to record daily, on a chart or on the board, one or more news items reported by the children, and to use them later in a reading period. Before an item is recorded, there is group discussion of the items that have been reported in order to determine which ones the children prefer to record. The reporting, the discussion of sentences, the organization, and the dictation of the news story to the teacher are valuable features of the daily language experiences of the group.

The second-grade teacher should continue the practice of having an informal news exchange or a show-and-tell period each

Our Trip
We went to the airport.
A man took us inside a plane.
Some men were working on the engine.
We saw one plane take off.
We saw a plane land.

A trip to an airport, reflected by the illustration at the opening of this chapter, resulted in various expressional activities. The story on the board is the part of the group account of the trip. One boy has drawn a picture of a special type of plane and is telling the group about it. One girl has found a story about airplanes and will find opportunity to read or tell it to the group.

day. Probably it should come in the opening minutes of the school day. The children may describe intriguing sights that they saw on the way home from school the previous day or on the way to school that very morning. Someone may have found a baby bird that had fallen from the nest; and, in the attempt to replace it, have had quite an experience with the excited parent birds. Another may have a visitor at home, perhaps a grandmother. A baby sister or brother may have arrived in the home of one boy or girl the day before.

For a show-and-tell period, one boy or girl may have brought a new book or toy to exhibit to interested classmates. One of the boys may have built a boat to sail in his wading pool. Such are the items that the children will present.

Informal Atmosphere The atmosphere for the news or the show-and-tell period should be as informal as possible, with girls and boys seated in their chairs in a semicircular group, or perhaps seated on a rug, with the teacher sitting on a low chair nearby. Individual children present their items, preferably not raising their hands for recognition before speaking. The teacher should be unobtrusively in control, inviting each child who is ready with news or an exhibit to take his turn. Yet always she should guide with the following objectives in mind:

To inspire voluntary expression by question and suggestion
To see that no child does more than his share of talking
To encourage a backward child to talk
To instill good listening habits
To lead children to question one another

As far as possible, she should let the children proceed without being conscious of outside direction. For the over-talkative child, however, there should be a quiet reminder; for the timid one, kindly and stimulating questions.

Usually the child's presentation will be quite brief; but there may be an occasion when one child will talk quite at length. He may have brought in a souvenir of a week-end trip to a seaside resort, or have received a pet whose tricks are many and varied. The nature of the news period will vary with the character of the items the children have to report.

The "show-and-tell" period provides opportunity for children to share their interests with the group. A girl tells about a character doll that she has dressed. A boy is ready to tell how he made a sailboat of which he is proud. Another boy will tell of his experiences with pet white mice. Oral expression motivated by personal interests usually frees the child of shyness or a feeling of inadequacy.

Corrective Work In such informal periods, the teacher will be on the alert to note the speech needs of the children, but will do little about them at the time. If some children do not keep their sentences apart (use too many *and*'s, *so*'s and *then*'s), if some words are incorrectly enunciated ("gonna" for *going to*, for example), if a gross and illiterate type of error is made ("youse," or *seen* for *saw*), the teacher will attempt to make the correct forms conspicuous through her own speech, in her oral reading, and through incorporation of the correct forms in reading charts. Through their listening and their oral reading, the children will also become familiar with the correct forms, which will soon sound right to their ears and eventually come naturally to their tongues. Particularly in the latter part of second grade, the teacher will plan often to have a language skills period later in the day, when the group will read and say the correct forms in practice sentences. To correct run-on sentences, she may have the children tell picture stories of two or three clear-cut sentences that have been thought out carefully before the child speaks, and then spoken in such manner as to show clearly where each sentence ends. In the case of a report that the teacher writes on the board, she calls attention to the correct form of a word or to correct sentence form.

However, there may be times, either in Grade One or Grade Two, when the teacher will make corrections within the news period. If a certain gross and illiterate type of error has received considerable attention in previous weeks, she may, during the news period, give immediate correction by saying, "You *saw* a jet plane, Jimmy. Say *saw*, not *seen*." This should be done quietly, in a manner that will not embarrass Jimmy or repress his desire to speak. Or, later, she may go quietly to Jimmy's side and say, "You forgot to say *I* saw this morning, Jimmy. Please tell me again what you *saw* last Sunday."

In Grade Two, practice lessons for a small group are appropriate for those children who have the same difficulty. Individual correction is in point for difficulties that are less prevalent, or for reminding a careless child of a correct form.

Reading Situations

Accompanying Language Values As indicated in the preceding chapter, reading lessons provide many and varied opportunities for talking. In both first and second grades, the reading of a story is ordinarily preceded either by guided group discussion of familiar stories that are similar in theme or development, or by stimulating children to recount experiences that will serve as background for the story to be read. In the second grade, new words are often introduced by writing them on the board in phrases or sentences lifted out of the story text. Their meaning is made clear before the pupils attempt to read the story.

After the story is read, various types of discussion may follow, in response to questions that (*a*) bear on the main steps in the story, (*b*) bring out significant details, (*c*) help the child to think sequentially, (*d*) make clear certain cause-and-effect relationships, or (*e*) center attention on new words that the group should incorporate in their vocabulary. Often the story will remind some children of other stories or of similar personal experiences that they wish to tell to their classmates.

The sentence concept may be strengthened by such questions as: "Find the sentence that tells where Jimmy went. Read it aloud"; or, "Find three sentences with the word *circus* in them. Read them aloud"; or, "Tell in one sentence what Joey found."

Dramatization A most valuable response to reading may be the informal dramatization of the story. A teacher interested in

Vicarious experiences through individual reading provide ideas and vocabulary for oral expression periods.

developing, within her group, such qualities as spontaneity, fluency, imagination, originality, and constructive social attitudes will frequently let them play their stories with little or no previous planning and with a minimum of direction.

Preferably the suggestion that the story be played should come from the group. If the action and conversation are simple enough, the children can proceed to choose a cast that will play the story. In more complex situations, there may be discussion of the setting of the story, of the principal train of events, and of the dialogue. Such informal dramatization is fun, and the spirit of spontaneity and enjoyment should not be dampened by criticism.

When time is available, more than one cast of characters may work out a dramatization. The second group may go to the hall, the cloakroom, or a far corner of the classroom to plan their own version of the play. Thus each cast is enabled to present their own conception of the story without being unduly influenced by the other cast of characters. Children who do not appear as actors will enjoy being the listening audience. They may at times help to appraise each presentation and to select a final cast, provided that the children wish to present their play to another class.

A Typical Dramatization One second-grade group proposed that they play "The Three Billy Goats Gruff," a story that they had just read. During the reading lesson there had been discussion of the action, and also dramatic reading of the conversational parts; therefore the teacher felt that more detailed planning would not be necessary, except to decide upon the making of a bridge.

Some children suggested that four chairs be placed side by side in the middle of the open space near the front of the room. One boy suggested that the sturdy worktable would make a better bridge because the troll could get under it. This latter suggestion was accepted, and a chair was placed at each end of the table to aid in mounting the bridge. Four volunteers acted the three scenes.

The group then evaluated the play, first expressing praise for the actors' modulation of voices to show the differences in the voices of the three goats and the troll. It was felt that there could be a more animated conversation between each pair of characters. So a second cast went through the dramatization, conversing in a livelier manner. It was then time for midmorning lunch, and the dramatization concluded for the time being. However, this favorite story was played again and again during free periods on subsequent days.

A simple dramatization, planned and executed by children, of the familiar story "The Three Billy Goats Gruff." Note the simply made horns worn by the goat characters and the mask of the ugly troll. Planning the dramatization motivated group discussion. Making the simple accessories occupied free-time activity and accompanying purposeful discussion. The simple dialogue comprised a recounting of the essence of the story, previously read by or to the children.

Dramatic Play   In dramatic play, a child impersonates someone else and so thoroughly identifies himself with the character that in his imagination he becomes that person. He thinks and behaves as if he were actually someone else.

Dramatic play ordinarily involves no story or plot. Children are engaging in dramatic play when they play school or store; when they dramatize Indians by sticking feathers in their hair; when they dress up in their parents' clothing and imitate their elders; when they pretend they are keeping house, running a store, or driving a fire truck, a bus or streetcar, or a racing automobile; when they set up a play post office and deliver mail. Young children spend much of their playtime at home in dramatic play. At school, there should be blocks for building an airport or a garage, dolls for playing house, some materials for costuming, toy trucks and drums, and other play materials that stimulate the children's imagination and encourage them to dramatize interesting activities in home or community. Such dramatic play may be pursued at recess time, if need be; better still, it may take place during free periods in the day's program.

The children in one beginning first grade came in from their morning play period and scattered to various interest centers around the large room. Four little girls went at once to a large wooden box from which they extracted some articles of clothing for an adult. They were soon garbed in long dresses and high-heeled pumps and carried big purses. One child was seated in the play-corner living room, ready to receive callers. When a knock came, she received her guests in a truly adult manner. Then there followed the kind of chitchat that they heard when their mothers had callers at home. Soon there was a serving of make-believe tea and cookies. Any mother, as well as any teacher in a modern first-grade classroom where children have some free playtime, can cite many similar incidents of boys and girls engaging voluntarily in dramatic play that momentarily seems very real to them.

Dramatic play has many values. To the child, it is a means of gaining an understanding of the adults he meets in his daily activities. Through his identification with them, he is taking strides toward becoming an intelligent and active member of a family and citizen in a community. Through dramatic play, the child learns about the common problems of group living, about fair play, and about the give-and-take of family living. Such play also develops the power of adjustment. Perhaps fully as important are the release of tensions and the expression of repressed feelings. To the teacher of the child, there are equivalent values. She may glimpse the tensions and problems that explain deviations in the behavior of individual children. Also revealed are the interests, special abilities, aptitudes, or needs of a child. The teacher can also see what language patterns the child is developing, and what he lacks in vocabulary and sentence mastery. She can help the boy or girl grow into a more stable, well-rounded personality if she is thus sensitive to the revelations of children's dramatic play.

Story and Poetry Hour

There should never be a day when the teacher fails to read or tell a story, to read aloud from a book that is being presented a chapter at a time, or to read and recite choice bits of verse to or with her pupils. The Story Hour should be a high light in the school day. The selection of story and verse should be varied so that the children may sometimes be highly amused, sometimes filled with enthusiastic approval, often curious, usually held by real suspense, and occasionally indignant. Imagination, or the ability to build mental pictures, should be stimulated by the literature that the teacher presents. Standards of conduct and ideals of human relationships may be instilled during such periods, and horizons of thought and insight gradually extended beyond the local community to peoples in faraway times and in distant places.

Teacher Preparation It is the practice of one successful and inspired teacher to shut herself away at times during a week to rehearse the reading she plans for the Story Hour. She knows that she must be thoroughly familiar with a story so that she may use the proper inflection to interpret ideas and emotions that characterize the story, and that she must catch the lilt, the rhyme, and the mood of a poem that she attempts to present to her group. Every teacher should hold herself responsible for such preparation. In fact, the teacher should be so thoroughly familiar with the text that she may seem to be telling the story herself or reciting the poem. Her eyes should meet the eyes of the children; her facial expression should reflect a response to the emotional situations in the various incidents in the story.

Much as children delight in hearing a story read, they gain even more enjoyment from the telling of a story. In fact, most stories should be told rather than read to the children. Only if the teacher cannot do justice to a story's unusual vocabulary or artistic style by telling it should she read it. A successful teacher of the first or second grade needs to have a rich repertoire of stories to tell. They are useful not only for the Story Hour, but also for those odd moments when, for some cause or other, a brief period of waiting occurs.

Selection of Poems The primary teacher should always have ready some poems to fit every occasion. If a child brings a wee turtle to school, she should be ready to present Vachel Lindsay's "The Little Turtle"; on the occasion of the first frost, she should read or recite a poem such as Laura Richards' "Jacky Frost." Always her choice should be made in relation to the maturity of her group. The thought should be simple and childlike and the rhythm marked, though sometimes rhyme may be lacking. Children love rhythm and lilt, and they often thoroughly enjoy a poem having unfamiliar words, provided always that the ideas and imagery are simple and childlike. In Elinor Wylie's "Velvet Shoes," for example, there are mood and imagery that recall the feeling of tiptoeing in a fresh, soft carpet of snow. Walter de la Mare's "Silver" makes the children visualize the silver-bathed night.

Children revel in words that portray sounds, such as the bell sounds in "Ding, Dong, Bell," or the sound of the ticking of the clock in "Hickory, Dickory, Dock." They delight in marked rhythms, such as the beat of horses' hoofs in—

> "Ride a cock-horse to Banbury Cross,
> To see an old lady upon a white horse."

or the rocking rhythm in—

> "Bye, baby bunting,
> Daddy's gone a-hunting."

They are also intrigued with marked rhyming. In searching for poetry for young children, therefore, the teacher must bear in mind the children's love of sound words and of marked rhythm and rhyming. Most of the Mother Goose rhymes embody these characteristics, and consequently they provide good introductory material for Grades One and Two. The list that follows includes a number of Mother Goose rhymes and also some other rhymes or verse for children. Most of them may be found in the anthologies and books of verse listed at the end of this chapter.

DRAMATIZATION

"Sing a Song of Sixpence"
"Wee Willie Winkie"
"Mix a Pancake," by Christina G. Rossetti
"Oh, Susan Blue," by Kate Greenaway

"The Egg," by Laura E. Richards
"Marching Song," by Robert Louis Stevenson
"The Balloon Man," by Dorothy Aldis
"The Picnic," by Dorothy Aldis
"Shore," by Mary B. Miller
"The Little Whistler," by Frances M. Frost
"Automobile Mechanics," by Dorothy Baruch
"Singing-Time," by Rose Fyleman
"The Christmas Pudding" (Mother Goose)
"Good Morning," by Muriel Sipe

RHYME

"The Swing," by Robert Louis Stevenson
"The Little Kittens," by Eliza Lee Follen
"As I Was Going Along, Along" (Mother Goose)
"The Three Foxes," by A. A. Milne
"The Buttercup Cow," by Elizabeth Rendall
"Holding Hands," by Lenora M. Link
"This Happy Day," by Harry Behn

ALLITERATION

"One Misty, Moisty Morning" (Mother Goose)
"Pat-a-Cake, Pat-a-Cake" (Mother Goose)
"Tired Tim," by Walter de la Mare
"Whistles," by Dorothy Aldis
"P's the Proud Policeman," by Phyllis McGinley
"C Is for the Circus," by Phyllis McGinley

RHYTHM

"This Is the Way the Ladies Ride" (Mother Goose)
"The Grand Old Duke of York" (Mother Goose)
"Master I Have" (Mother Goose)

"Little Wind," by Kate Greenaway
"The Mitten Song," by Marie Louise Allen
"Husky Hi," by Rose Fyleman
"Hoppity," by A. A. Milne
"The Cupboard," by Walter de la Mare
"The Jolly Woodchuck," by Marion Edey
"B's the Bus," by Phyllis McGinley
"E Is the Escalator," by Phyllis McGinley

MOTION

"Merry-Go-Round," by Dorothy Baruch
"Grandfather Frog," Louise S. Bechtel
"The New Baby Calf," by Edith H. Newlin
"Jump—Jump—Jump," by Kate Greenaway
"Windy Wash Day," by Dorothy Aldis
"The Little Turtle," by Vachel Lindsay

SENSORY APPEAL

"Smells," by Christopher Morley
"Ice," by Dorothy Aldis
"Galoshes," by Rhoda W. Bacmeister ✓
"It is Raining," by Lucy Sprague Mitchell
"The White Window," by James Stephens
"The Barnyard," by Maude Burnham
"What Is It?" by Marie Louise Allen
"Trains at Night," by Frances M. Frost
"Aeroplane," by Mary McB. Green
"Stop—Go," by Dorothy Baruch
"The Baby Goes to Boston," by Laura E. Richards
"The Big Clock," Author Unknown
"My Valentine," by Mary C. Parsons

IMAGINATION

"Us Two," by A. A. Milne
"Hiding," by Dorothy Aldis
"Our Circus," by Laura L. Randall
"The Cat's Tea-Party," by Frederick E. Weatherly
"My Donkey," by Rose Fyleman

During the Story Hour, the teacher should read poems in such a manner as to portray the enjoyable features of each. Several poems related to a current interest may be read at one period. When a unit related to farm life is in progress, Stevenson's "The Cow" and Elizabeth Madox Roberts' "The Hens" may be read. After the children have engaged in dramatic play during a free period, the teacher may read Stevenson's "A Good Play" and Dorothy Aldis' "Hiding."

Source of Materials   No teacher's professional library is complete without some collections of poetry and story. Among the many available are the excellent volumes listed at the close of this chapter. As the teacher discovers poems and stories suited to special occasions and uses, she will find it desirable to make them available for use from year to year. Making a classified list of poems and stories, with references to sources, is one way of doing this. A still better device is to keep a classified file drawer containing cards or sheets of paper on which stories and poems for specific occasions are written or typed. Such a device will enable the teacher to select the right poem for any occasion at a moment's notice. A loose-leaf scrapbook is another means.

Memorization   There should probably be no definite attempt to have children in the first and second grades memorize poetry. However, their impressionable minds will absorb much verse as they hear again and again those favorite bits of verse that they like most. Christopher Morley's "Animal Crackers," Vachel Lindsay's "The Moon's the North Wind's Cooky," and lines from *Winnie-the-Pooh,* by A. A. Milne, are likely candidates for this effortless memorization.

Communication in a Constructional Activities Period

Many teachers do not realize the importance of one of the vital features of the language curriculum. This is the conversation that children engage in when they are busy with crafts, art work, and constructional activities involved in the modern experience curriculum. Unless most of the children are engaged in study or in reading activities when quiet is essential, it is inadvisable to repress exchange of ideas among the children who are engaged in manual activities. True, they must show self-control and a disposition to be orderly; but quiet, purposeful, friendly conversation and discussion during creative activities should usually be permitted and even encouraged.

All experience units involve much *doing* by the children. During such active part of the learning process, the children should discuss quietly the next steps in carrying out the group plans, or some problems related to the use of equipment. Several children may be busy at a mural showing the experiences of a trip to a dairy farm, while others work on a bulletin-board display of dairy products used for food. Still others may be setting up a model farm on a nearby table. Such constructional activities offer opportunities for purposeful and spontaneous expression. Social adjustments are made as children shed their shyness or subdue their excessive aggressiveness. Their expression is natural, informal, and purposeful: and the teacher may determine needs for improvement in enunciation or enrichment of vocabulary.

Values in Language Improvement   There is no type of language expression that has a more truly socializing influence than has the one under consideration. Children offer one another helpful suggestions; they give and take directions or offer and accept assistance in the interest of improving their product. The plans that have been made in group discussion are talked over and modified as needed. There are small group conferences and subsequent explanations of those modifications that have proved necessary. In a classroom where all the children are busy with various art or creative enterprises, there may even be conversation about a party, a game, a new pet, and other personal topics.

Teacher Survey   The teacher who knows how to keep all her children profitably busy with their hands while they quietly converse or discuss topics of interest gains rich dividends in language improvement. She learns much about the established and developing interests of her children. Their grasp of the sentence, the breadth or poverty of their vocabulary, the presence of speech difficulties or of gross errors in word usage, and their social as well as emotional adjustment are all revealed as she moves from group to group. Such a period is a real opportunity for the teacher to know her children better and to learn how to utilize their interests and meet their language needs.

Attention to Skills

In informal types of oral communication that constitute spontaneous expression, the child is engrossed in the ideas he is expressing, and he may consequently have little regard for the forms and technicalities of language. Even so, the fluency and purposefulness in such expression are desirable goals of language instructions, and they are likely to make for effectiveness. Aside from incidental correction of gross errors on the part of individual pupils, the teacher does little within such an expressional period to improve the form of expression except through her own good example in directness of manner, clarity of enunciation, clear-cut sentence structure, use of vocabulary, and the like. It is through imitation of the teacher as model in all respects that much of the improvement in children's expression comes.

When some or all of the group need help in correcting specific errors and weaknesses, the teacher should schedule periods occasionally to give practice in skills, such as speaking in complete sentences, enunciating correctly and clearly, and choosing the correct word form to replace an incorrect one. These periods of direct teaching will be discussed in Chapters 4 and 6.

Bibliography

ANNOTATED BOOK LISTS

A Basic Book Collection for Elementary Grades. Issued by the American Library Association, 50 East Huron Street, Chicago 11

A Bibliography of Books for Children. Issued by the Association for Childhood Education International, 1200 Fifteenth Street, Northwest, Washington 5, D. C.

EATON, ANNE THAXTER. *Treasure for the Taking.* The Viking Press, Inc., New York 17

STORY ANTHOLOGIES

Told under the Blue Umbrella, Told under the Green Umbrella, Told under the Magic Umbrella, and *Told under the Stars and Stripes.* Four volumes of stories selected by the Literature Committee of the Association for Childhood Education International. The Macmillan Company, New York 11

With Cap and Bells and *Baker's Dozen*. Edited by Mary Gould Davis. Harcourt, Brace and Company, Inc., New York 17

Favorite Stories Old and New. Edited by Sidonie Matsner Gruenberg. Doubleday and Company, Inc., Garden City, New York

PYLE, HOWARD. *The Wonder Clock*. E. M. Hale and Company, Eau Claire, Wisconsin

POETRY ANTHOLOGIES

Time for Poetry. Compiled by May Hill Arbuthnot. Scott, Foresman and Company, Chicago 11

Sung under the Silver Umbrella and *Sung under the Blue Umbrella*. Selected by the Literature Committee of the Association for Childhood Education International. The Macmillan Company, New York 11

Poems for the Children's Hour. Compiled by Josephine Bouton. Platt and Monk, Inc., New York 10

Bridled with Rainbows. Compiled by Sara and John E. Brewton. (See also *Gaily We Parade* and *Under the Tent of the Sky*, compiled by John E. Brewton.) The Macmillan Company, New York 11

A Small Child's Book of Verse. Compiled by Pelagie Doane. Oxford University Press, New York 11

A Treasury of Verse for Little Children. Compiled by M. G. Edgar. Thomas Y. Crowell Company, New York 16

Very Young Verses. Compiled by Barbara P. Geismer and Antoinette B. Suter. Houghton Mifflin Company, Boston 7

The Golden Flute. Compiled by Alice Hubbard and Adeline Babbitt. The John Day Company, New York 36

Chimney Corner Poems. Edited by Veronica Hutchinson. G. P. Putnam's Sons, New York 16

For a Child: Great Poems Old and New. Edited by Wilma McFarland. The Westminster Press, Philadelphia 7

Rainbow in the Sky. Edited by Louis Untermeyer. Harcourt, Brace and Company, New York 17

BOOKS OF VERSE

ALDIS, DOROTHY. *All Together.* G. P. Putnam's Sons, New York 16

BEHN, HARRY. *The Little Hill* and *Windy Morning.* Harcourt, Brace and Company, New York 17

CHUTE, MARCHETTE. *Rhymes about the City* and *Rhymes about the Country.* The Macmillan Company, New York 11

CLARK, ANNE NOLAN. *In My Mother's House.* The Viking Press, Inc., New York 17

COATSWORTH, ELIZABETH. *Summer Green.* The Macmillan Company, New York 11

DE LA MARE, WALTER. *Rhymes and Verses: Collected Poems for Children.* Henry Holt and Company, Inc., New York 17

FIELD, RACHEL. *Taxis and Toadstools,* Doubleday and Company, Inc., Garden City, New York

FROST, FRANCES. *The Little Whistler.* Whittlesey House Publication, McGraw-Hill Book Company, New York 36

MILNE, A. A. *Now We Are Six* and *When We Were Very Young.* E. P. Dutton and Company, Inc., New York 10

ROBERTS, ELIZABETH MADOX. *Under the Tree.* The Viking Press, Inc., New York 17

ROBINSON, TOM. *In and Out.* The Viking Press, Inc., New York 17

STEVENSON, ROBERT LOUIS. *A Child's Garden of Verses.* Charles Scribner's Sons, New York 17

TIPPETT, J. S. *I Go A-Traveling; I Live in a City;* and *I Know Some Little Animals.* Harper and Brothers, New York 16

GENERAL ANTHOLOGIES

The Arbuthnot Anthology of Children's Literature. Compiled by May Hill Arbuthnot. (Includes *Time for Poetry* in preceding list.) Scott, Foresman and Company, Chicago 11

A Book of Children's Literature. Edited by Lillian Hollowell. Rinehart and Company, Inc., New York 16

Story and Verse for Children. Edited by Miriam Blanton Huber. The Macmillan Company, New York 11

Anthology of Children's Literature. Compiled by Edna Johnson, Carrie Scott, and Evelyn Sickels. Houghton Mifflin Company, Boston 7

STORIES OF MAKE-BELIEVE

BACON, PEGGY. *The Lion-Hearted Kitten, and Other Stories.* The Macmillan Company, New York 11

BANNERMAN, HELEN. *The Story of Little Black Sambo.* J. B. Lippincott Company, Philadelphia 5

BIANCO, MARGERY. *The Velveteen Rabbit.* Doubleday and Company, Inc., Garden City, New York

BONTEMPS, ARNA, and CONROY, JACK. *The Fast Sooner Hound.* Houghton Mifflin Company, Boston 7

BROCK, EMMA L. *The Runaway Sardine* and *To Market! To Market!* Alfred A. Knopf, Inc., New York 22

BURTON, VIRGINIA LEE. *Choo Choo* and *Mike Mulligan and His Steam Shovel.* Houghton Mifflin Company, Boston 7

CHALMERS, AUDREY. *Hundreds and Hundreds of Pancakes.* The Viking Press, Inc., New York 17

FLACK, MARJORIE. *Ask Mr. Bear.* The Macmillan Company, New York 11

FREEMAN, LYDIA and DON. *Pet of the Met.* The Viking Press, Inc., New York 17

GÁG, WANDA. *Millions of Cats* and *Nothing-at-All.* Coward-McCann, Inc., New York 16

GRAMATKY, HARDIE. *Little Toot* and *Loopy.* G. P. Putnam's Sons, New York 16

MEIGS, CORNELIA. *The Wonderful Locomotive.* The Macmillan Company, New York 11

MILNE, A. A. *The House at Pooh Corner* and *Winnie-the-Pooh.* E. P. Dutton and Company, Inc., New York 10

POTTER, BEATRIX. *The Tale of Peter Rabbit.* Frederick Warne and Company, Inc., New York 10

SEUSS, DR. (Pseudonym of Theodor Seuss Geisel). *And to Think That I Saw It on Mulberry Street* and *The 500 Hats of Bartholomew Cubbins.* Vanguard Press, New York 17

SLOBODKIN, LOUIS. *Circus April 1st.* The Macmillan Company, New York 11

TREGARTHEN, ENYS (Pseudonym of Nellie Sloggett). *The Doll Who Came Alive.* The John Day Company, New York 36

INFORMATIONAL BOOKS

BARUCH, DOROTHY. *Big Fellow.* E. M. Hale and Company, Eau Claire, Wisconsin

BESKOW, ELSA. *Pelle's New Suit.* Harper and Brothers, New York 16

BURTON, VIRGINIA LEE. *Katy and the Big Snow* and *The Little House.* Houghton Mifflin Company, Boston 7

DALGLEISH, ALICE. *America Travels.* The Macmillan Company, New York 11

GRAMATKY, HARDIE. *Hercules: The Story of an Old-Fashioned Fire Engine.* G. P. Putnam's Sons, New York 16

HADER, BERTA and ELMER. *Little Town.* The Macmillan Company, New York 11

HUBER, MIRIAM. *Cinder, the Cat* and *Skags, the Milk Horse.* American Book Company, New York 3

LENSKI, LOIS. *We Live in the City.* J. B. Lippincott Company, Philadelphia 5

LENT, HENRY B. *Diggers and Builders.* The Macmillan Company, New York 11

POLITI, LEO. *A Boat for Peppe.* Charles Scribner's Sons, New York 17

The More Organized Forms of Oral Communication

CHAPTER 4

In general, the more organized forms of communication are allocated to the second grade, since first-grade children have not yet developed to the stage where they have either the necessary length of attention span or the organizing ability to carry on the more organized expressional activities. However, in most first grades there will be a few comparatively mature children who can do as well as some children in a second-grade group; and, toward the end of the year, a number of girls and boys in the first grade can participate effectively in several phases of organized oral communication.

The judgment of the teacher, therefore, must determine which types of language activity presented in this chapter are adapted to the children in her group.

Picture Stories

Children enjoy looking at meaningful pictures that portray action and represent experiences that they are able to interpret and enjoy. Story pictures about children, their pets, wildlife in field and forest and zoo, and family situations are especially interesting. Very interesting language can be centered about such pictures, which many teachers collect by clipping appropriate colored advertisements and covers from magazines. In discussing a picture, the teacher can purposely introduce a new word that the children might well add to their speaking vocabulary. She can encourage the children in the group to suggest suitable words to describe persons, objects, or action in the picture. She can strengthen the sentence concept by having the children take turns telling one, two, or three sentences about the picture. If more than one sentence is requested, the exercise may be used to emphasize the necessity of keeping sentences apart—not stringing them together with *and*'s, *so*'s, and *then*'s.

Storytelling based on pictures is also an effective means of providing practice in sequential thinking or simple organization of ideas. As children grasp the situation portrayed in a picture, they can be led to imagine what has just happened to precipitate that situation, and what must be the logical conclusion to it. In other words, a story that is suggested by a picture will answer the following questions: (1) What do you think has just happened? (2) What is happening right now? (3) What is going to happen? or how will it end? These questions should not be asked in a stilted or routine way; but the children can be led to see that there must be a definite beginning and ending to a story, such as may be suggested by questions 1 and 3 above. This is one of the simplest ways of developing the idea of sequential order in story organization. It also aids in the development of the sentence concept.

Sometimes there may be a single large picture for which all the children think up a story. Often there should be several striking pictures displayed on a bulletin board or on a flannel board. Each child may select the picture that is most interesting to him and compose a story about it. At times the children may bring in enough pictures to permit each child to have one for himself.

In a second grade in which children were having considerable trouble with run-on sentences, the teacher brought in several large colored pictures that she had clipped from magazines. She said, "Here are some pictures of fun you may have with your pets. Look at them a minute, and choose the one you like best. Then we'll talk about the pictures you like."

As usual, most of the children joined their sentences with *and*'s as they talked. The teacher then said, "I am glad that you like these pictures. How would each of you like to tell a short story about the picture you like best? Think of your story now. As you plan, think of the three things you want to say. Then plan to use only three sentences. As you tell your own story, be sure to say each sentence by itself. We will listen to make sure how many sentences you have used." Here are the stories told by two children about the pictures they had chosen:

(1)

Billy threw the ball over the doghouse. Spot jumped right over the doghouse after the ball. He ran back to Billy with the ball.

(2)

Sally's new bicycle is a birthday present. Her father put a basket on the bicycle. Sally's little dog can go riding in it.

Each story is truly an original composition, since it relates what the child imagined about a pictured episode.

The illustration at the opening of this chapter shows a group of children outdoors, observing the natural phenomena of fall and gathering specimens of colorful leaves, seed pods, cocoons, nests, and other items of interest to them. The experiences were part of a science study. They resulted in the setting up of a science exhibit, with attendant preliminary discussion as to selection of specimens, arrangement, and the printing of labels.

Discussing Plans for a Group Story

In Grade One, the teacher should stimulate and guide a discussion of the facts and ideas that are to be incorporated in the experience story. She should also guide the children in selecting from among the sentences that are volunteered, and in arranging them in a simple, clear-cut, and orderly presentation of the pupils' experience. In the latter part of the first grade or early in the second grade, the more advanced children will be able to write a few sentences independently. However, even in Grade

Two, much of the writing will be done by the teacher as children dictate to her the story of a group or an individual experience. In the first grade, the sentences will, in general, be short and few in number, as in the story that follows.

The Bakery

We went to the bakery.
We saw the ovens.
There was bread in them.
The baker gave each
     of us a little loaf.
It was very good.

After a visit to a neighborhood bakery, a first-grade group planned and dictated this story of their experiences. The orderly sequence of ideas is evidence of the careful planning and discussion that preceded the dictation of the story to the teacher.

Second-grade children can take considerable responsibility for deciding what facts and ideas to tell and for determining their sequential order in the story. As they struggle to construct their sentences, the group will engage in thoughtful discussion of the more organized type; that is, in discussion toward definite ends.

Here is a discussion of plans for a group story about a trip to a train:

SUE. Miss Lane, may we write a story about our visit to the train? I would like to put the story in my train book.

BILLY. Oh, yes. May we, Miss Lane? I'd like to read our story to Father and Mother.

MISS LANE. Sue and Billy have a good idea, haven't they? If you will all think hard about what you wish to say, I'll write your story on the board. What title do you want to use for the story?

JIMMY. We Visit a Train.

MISS LANE. Do you all like that title? (*The children agree that they do, and Miss Lane writes the title on the board.*) Now, what do you want to say first? What will your first sentence be? (*Several sentences are suggested, but they are not accepted by the class.*)

SUE. Friday morning we went to visit a train. (*This sentence is accepted by the class, and Miss Lane writes it.*)

MISS LANE. What will your next sentence be?

JIMMY (*after several others have suggested sentences*). It was standing on a sidetrack. (*The class accepts this sentence.*)

MISS LANE. What next? How did the train happen to be on the sidetrack? (*After various suggestions, the following sentences are accepted by the class.*)

TED. The train stays there all day.

BILLY. Some men get it ready for the next night trip.

ANNE. It must be ready to leave at four o'clock. (*And so the story goes on.*)

Specific Values in Terms of Language Ability It is obvious that the writing of a co-operative story of this kind calls, first of all, for thoughtful oral expression. It will involve such experiences in thinking and expression as:

Deciding which events or ideas to include
Determining the correct sequence of events or ideas
Building a sentence to express each thought
Choosing the exact words to convey thought
Using correct word forms

The co-operative story thus develops orderly thinking and discussion and also entails language values that will function in independent story-writing later.

In addition, when the children copy the story, there will be concentration on writing skills including capitalization, punctuation, and spelling. It is important that, from the beginning of practical writing, children try to use such mechanics correctly. The co-operative story promotes such learnings when the teacher, as she writes the sentences on the board, frequently calls attention to the end-punctuation for sentences and to the use of capital letters wherever they are needed.

Giving and Interpreting Directions

In the modern classroom program, there are many occasions for the children to receive and interpret directions, instructions, and explanations, and to give them to classmates as well. To be effective, these types of communication must be well organized. Planning ahead of time is essential.

Listening to and Following Directions Experiences in listening to, interpreting, and following directions may be afforded at almost any period in the day if the teacher will but see the opportunity and use it to advance language training. Children love to assist the teacher, and they are only too glad to be called upon for such assistance as is indicated by directions such as those that follow:

"John, please open the top right-hand drawer in my desk. Find the green notebook and bring it to me."

"Beth, please go to the bookcase. Find the six copies of *Here and There with Henry*. Then pass them out to the reading group."

The children study a picture, each one trying to weave a story about it. After each child has told his story, the teacher will read the story that the picture illustrates.

Such directions, *given only once,* accustom the children to attentive listening and thoughtful interpretation. Should John or Beth fail to pass the test of attention and interpretation, the teacher should ask another child to follow the directions. But she should seek an early opportunity to put John or Beth to similar tests until the child is able to listen, interpret, and execute correctly at a single telling—an ability that is based on good listening and organized thinking. As reading ability develops, simple directions may be written on the board.

It is the tendency of the busy teacher to do too much herself and to fail to seize opportunities to develop good listening habits, self-reliance, and a sense of real responsibility on the part of the children. Again, a teacher may tend to over-assist the child who is called upon to help, or to repeat directions several times, or to give directions only to those who have already proved that they can interpret and execute them most readily. She should, of course, keep in mind the other children who most need to gain proficiency in following directions, and should give them frequent opportunities to listen to and carry out directions. In harmony with the conception of the language program as a daylong activity, the teacher must look upon every opportunity for communication as a feature of the language program and therefore utilize the giving of directions, instructions, and explanations, both by herself and by the children, as opportunities for increasing the children's ability to listen, to interpret, to think, and to express.

Directions by the Child   As for the child, complete familiarity with a process is necessary if his own directions, instructions, or explanations are to be clear. If he is explaining to the group how to hold a hammer correctly, the technique will probably be demonstrated. At the same time, he will give verbal directions and explain why a certain manner of holding the hammer is preferable. The demonstration and parallel instructions would be impossible if the young instructor had not learned through actual experience how to hold the tool.

It is necessary for the child to keep his listeners in mind when planning and giving instructions or directions. For instance, when he is trying to tell a new teacher how to reach his home for a call upon his mother, the child must be very exact. He must know the names of streets, the number of blocks to go in each successive direction, and the location of key buildings or stop lights that may act as guideposts along the way. If he bungles in his first effort to give his teacher the correct directions, the teacher may suggest that he start anew after thinking through a clear-cut set of directions.

After observing his father plant some bulbs, the child may take responsibility of telling classmates how to make plantings in preparation for Mother's Day, when each child wishes to take a potted plant home. Again, he must plan how to instruct his fellows; he must speak in sentences that clearly convey his meaning; and the sentences must be in the right order.

It is not easy to give instructions, directions, or explanations— not even for the teacher or for any adult. Doing so in a satisfactory way calls for careful planning. Children gladly accept the challenge to be effective in these types of communication when there is something to be accomplished through engaging in them. Granted a worthwhile end and the chance to be thoroughly familiar with a process, a child can do a good job.

Reports on Observations

In first or second grade, a report is usually informal. For example, one child may have seen a newly arrived bird in spring, and he describes it in detail so that his classmates or the teacher can identify it.

Another may have watched a group of workers near his home paving a side street, and he explains the process or procedure he has observed to his interested audience (who may thus be stimulated to plan a trip to see these same street workers).

In general, there is less giving of individual reports in the first grade than in the second.

Directed Observation   In presenting such a report, there is a demand for a certain degree of organization of materials. However, the organization will grow out of the nature of the topic or experience upon which the report is based. In reporting on the bird, for example, the child should sense the need for describing color, size, song or call, actions or nest-building technique; for telling where the bird was seen; and for giving other distinguishing characteristics or facts if he wishes his hearers to identify the bird from his description.

To develop the children's sense of organization, the teacher will plan special periods for observation, sometimes of objects or pets brought into the classroom and sometimes through observation trips outdoors. In preparation, she will raise questions designed to direct the children's observation, or stimulate the group to raise them. On a first trip to observe spring birds, the group may be directed in discussing what to look for and in listing questions like the following:

> What color is the bird?
> Is he as big as a robin?
> What is he doing?
> What kind of song or call has he?
> What kind of nest is he building?

If children are to observe (study) an abandoned oriole's nest brought into the classroom in fall, questions like the following may be raised:

> What is the nest made of?
> How are the materials put together?
> What size is it?   What shape is it?
> What bird builds this kind of nest?

When the children grow accustomed to organized observation, they will develop the habit of organized reporting.

The Report By the second half of the year, a second-grade child should plan an occasional individual report. Perhaps he is to tell about the progress of his committee in carrying out an enterprise assigned to them by the class. He will probably organize his report in terms of the sequence of the committee's activities and conclude with a statement of things still to be accomplished. Sometimes a child may report on an out-of-school experience. Again, he must report according to sequence. In fact, the main type of organization that may be expected of young children will be the sequential type.

A girl in the second grade had just returned from a winter in Florida. One of her most exciting experiences had been the opportunity to sleep in an upper berth. Upon her mention of this fact, her classmates asked her to tell all about it, or to "make a report." This is what the child said about her experience:

> On the train I slept in an upper berth. I watched the porter make it up. First he pulled down a shelf that was up against the ceiling of the coach. It had pillows and blankets on it. He used some of these to make Mother's bed in the lower berth. The others he used to make my bed. When the bed was ready, the porter brought a little ladder and I climbed up. It was fun to sleep so high up.

Discussion toward Specific Ends

The discussion that precedes a reading lesson or that occurs during the oral exchange of news items may be quite informal. Often it is really more like conversation than discussion. The contrary is true when a group is discussing definite plans for carrying on some activity.

Planning a Group Enterprise In planning a trip to visit a dairy farm, for example, the discussion must be pointed toward definite ends. The procedure in the second grade might be as follows:

> TEACHER (*raising questions to stimulate thought and discussion*). If we wish to visit Mr. Lane's dairy farm, what plans must we make? (*Children make various suggestions.*)

> JIMMY. I think we ought to make a list of things we have to do.

The class accept Jimmy's suggestion and proceed to discuss ways and means. The following list, dictated (under teacher guidance) by the children and written on the board by the teacher, is a written language outcome of the discussion:

Plans for Our Trip

1 Write a note to our principal asking permission to visit the dairy farm.
2 Write a class note to Mr. Lane to find out when we may visit his farm.
3 Find out which fathers or mothers will take us and bring us back.
4 List questions to ask Mr. Lane at his farm.
5 Divide the questions among us.
6 Make some safety rules for the trip.
7 Make some courtesy rules.

Then there follows some discussion of each of the items, the teacher suggesting it as follows:

> TEACHER. Now that we have our list of what we must do, which point must we discuss first?

Language Values   Naturally, all the listed points will not be handled in one period. Item 1 would probably be the first point, and discussing and composing the note will occupy one written language period. Copying it may occupy another; so with most of the other steps in planning.

Organized discussion of the kind indicated above provides definite training in discussion and in organization of ideas in that it requires the child to:

1   Think about a definite point and then stick to it in discussion.
2   Feel responsible for contributing to the discussion.
3   Contribute something of value whenever he speaks.
4   State his ideas clearly if he expects them to be considered by the group.
5   Listen thoughtfully to each speaker.
6   Take his turn, and not monopolize.

By-products in Other Types of Expression   Notice the many language by-products in opportunities for further expressional work to be carried on in later periods: (*a*) planning, dictating, and copying a class note; (*b*) planning and copying a class letter; (*c*) discussing and listing questions to guide observation; (*d*) discussing, composing, and listing safety and courtesy rules. Also, observe (*e*) that the concept of the sentence (the *complete thought* idea) is strengthened by such activities as composing sentences for the note and the letter, and listing plans, questions, or rules; (*f*) that the teacher's writing of the children's sentences on the board reviews again and again the correct form for writing statements, commands, and questions; and (*g*) that the children have motivated practice in capitalization, punctuation, spelling, and writing while copying notes, letters, and rules from the board.

Dramatization or Storytelling for an Assembly

Informal storytelling and the dramatization of stories call for originality and spontaneity. Therefore, even in Grade Two, informal presentation should receive greater emphasis than a more formal type that involves planning in considerable detail and rehearsing before presentation. However, before the end of the second grade, the group should at some time have experience in presenting a planned and rehearsed play or story in an assembly or some other formal program. Such a presentation calls for careful diction and articulation, clarity of tone, ease of manner, and other qualities of finished, public presentation. In life outside school, there are occasional demands for public appearances of children in connection with religious, community, and social organizations. There should, therefore, be some attention to special-occasion appearances in the language curriculum of the school. The preparation of a play and a story for an assembly affords such experience.

Planned Dramatization　A planned dramatization may be discussed in detail and rehearsed until it becomes a finished product. In planning the play, several or all of the following steps should be worked out through discussion:

1　Divide the story into scenes or acts, and name each part.
2　List the characters in each act or each scene.

3 Discuss time, place, and setting in connection with each scene or act.

4 Determine the scenery, action, and probable conversation for the first scene or act.

5 Choose a cast for the first tryout.

6 After the tryout, let the group give constructive suggestions and choose another cast for a second tryout.

7 Repeat steps 4, 5, and 6 for each scene of the play.

8 Let the group choose the final cast.

9 Discuss costuming, scenery, and properties in connection with each scene or act. Choose committees to be responsible for preparing or securing whatever is necessary.

There are degrees of formality, and almost any of the steps above may be omitted. Experienced teachers have learned that young children tire of dramatization that is unduly formal in its preparation.

There is little justification for having children memorize a ready-made play such as may be found in some periodicals and books. It is far better for the children to plan their own play from an original story or from a story in their readers or in a storybook. The work of planning gives group experience in organizing ideas as to background and action, and in creating dialogue appropriate to characters and action. Such planning also gives opportunity for vital discussion, for thoughtful evaluation, and for careful rereading of the story.

As the children plan their play and try out the various scenes, they find cause to revise, to iron out impossible situations, and to add intriguing complications. The resourcefulness and originality called for by such revisions constitute one of the main values of using pupil-planned plays rather than those printed in books and magazines.

Planned Storytelling Often the story selected for presentation in an assembly will be an account of a group or personal experience—one that is entirely new to the audience. It may sometimes be the retelling of a favorite story from a book. Imaginative children should be encouraged to create a story. In preparation, the storyteller, with the counsel and assistance of teacher and classmates, will be responsible for most of the following steps:

1 Selecting an experience or story that is interesting and full of fast-moving action
2 Thinking through the step-by-step development of the story
3 Planning a beginning that will catch interest and attention
4 Choosing vivid words that will create mental pictures in the listeners
5 Rehearsing the story before classmates to get suggestions for improvement
6 Improving the story until it can be told with ease and fluency

Second-grade children should not rehearse often. Two or three preliminary tellings before the teacher or the homeroom audience should be enough. Help the child to keep in mind such standards as the following:

How to Tell a Story

1 Speak each word distinctly.
2 Keep sentences apart (do not string them together with and's or so's).
3 Look at the audience.
4 Show interest in your own story.

Occasionally a second grade will present a simple report at an assembly. It may be an account of a group enterprise, presented by several children, each reporting on a phase of it. The steps in preparing for such a report are similar to those in preparing a story.

Choral Speaking

In the first and second grades, scarcely a day will pass without the teacher's reading a poem or two to her children. Such poems may be suggested by the fact that the circus is opening in the town, by something displayed in the show-and-tell period, by a rainy day, by the first snow, or by the new kittens of Billy's cat. Sometimes it will be fun for the group just to listen to a nonsense rhyme or to say some familiar nursery rhymes together.

Almost always, a group of children will have favorite poems for which they ask again and again. Usually, after three or four hearings, they begin to say parts of such poems with the teacher as she repeats the familiar lines. Thus choral speaking may begin.

Values In the first and second grades, *group speaking* or *verse choir* would probably be a more suitable term than is the customary title of *choral speaking*. There should be no attempt to achieve the finished performances. Instead, the children say their favorite verses together because they find it fun to do so.

Choral speaking of this informal type makes an important contribution to the social aspect of the language arts program by providing a strong impetus toward group co-operation. Children readily realize that verse speaking is not successful unless every child in the group makes a strong effort to harmonize his voice and speech with those of the rest of the group. Furthermore, the timid individual is permitted to feel very much a part of the group, and to exercise his speech arts without self-consciousness, such as might attend his individual effort to read or recite a poem; and the habits of speech and voice control developed in his choral speaking are likely to carry over into his daily speech.

Furthermore, choral speaking makes a strong contribution to reading and literature, which are definitely a part of the language arts program. If choral speaking is to be successful, children must (*a*) understand, mentally as well as emotionally, the thought of the poet's lines; (*b*) appreciate the connotation and also the music of his words; (*c*) feel the rhythm of the meter; and (*d*) enjoy the music of rhyme. The extent to which a child appreciates literary writing in all these aspects will determine the extent to which he later reads literature with real pleasure.

Types of Group Speaking Three types of group speaking are especially appropriate for young children. One is the *refrain* type in which the teacher speaks most of a stanza alone, with the children joining in on a refrain, such as "Dinkums, dunkums, little gray billy goat." Another easy one is the *line-a-child* or *line-a-group* type in which each line or couplet is spoken by a different pupil or small group. "One, two, buckle my shoe" is a jingle of this type. The third type is the *antiphonal*, in which two groups speak in turn, one saying a question and the other giving the answer as in "Pussy-cat, Pussy-cat, Where Have You Been?"

Of all the types of choral speaking, *unison* is the most difficult. It is hard to get many voices to blend smoothly. Unison speaking is, therefore, stressed more at the upper grade or high school level. However, because children get so much enjoyment and such fine social experience out of unison speaking of familiar nursery rhymes, the teacher of first or second grade may advisedly allow children to say their favorite ones together.

The Song Approach In the second grade, one way to approach choral speaking is through familiar songs that children enjoy singing. In preparation, the teacher herself should analyze the stanzas of several songs to determine how to divide them into thought units. A good beginning song is one with a refrain, or chorus. When the children next ask to sing that song, the teacher might suggest: "Would you like to turn yourselves into a choir? In a choir, some of the singers sing one part of the song, and some sing another. Would you like to have the girls sing the stanzas and the boys sing the chorus?"

Children will enjoy playing choir. The division of the song between boys and girls is an easy one as a starter, and the simple two-part arrangement provides a first step toward correct *timing* —a factor that is important in choral speaking and one that requires group co-operation.

After the group succeeds with that song and learns to time well, a familiar song like the following old lullaby may be attempted:

A LULLABY

Group I   { Hush-a-by, hush-a-by,
                 { Go to sleep, dear.

Group II   { Hush-a-by, hush-a-by,
                 { Mother is here.

Group III { She will not leave you,
                 { She will be near,

Group IV   { Hush-a-by, hush-a-by,
                 { Go to sleep, dear!

For this song, the choir may be divided into four groups, as shown. After the groups have identified their lines and have succeeded in timing correctly, the new factor of voice quality may be introduced, as follows: "When Mother sings Baby to sleep, haven't you noticed that she sings more softly when his eyelids begin to droop? When we sing the lullaby, shouldn't each group sing a little more softly than the group before it?"

The lullaby may then be sung several times until each group has sensed the proper gradation in volume of voice.

At this time, also, it may be well to think of individual voices and make a first attempt to secure complete unity of sound. The group voice should sound as a single voice; no one child's voice should be recognizable, or "stand out." If this can be achieved in part singing, a good start on attaining the same end with the speech choir will have been made. Judgment and comment as to the single-voice effect of the singing group should be secured from the group or groups not singing. The latter groups can be asked to listen closely to the singing group, so that they can appraise their performance through answering such questions as: Did Group I sound like a single voice? Could you hear any one child? Was the group voice (*a*) pleasing? (*b*) too loud? (*c*) too soft? Did the tone of voice suit the words of the song?

In the case of the child whose voice can be distinguished above the group voice, comment should be tactful. It is a good plan to give the child a whispered suggestion to keep quiet at first and listen to the group tone; then let him join in when he thinks he can blend his voice with the tone of the group.

Use of Jingles In passing from the singing choir to the verse choir, it is well to begin with very simple rhymes. In the speech text *This Way to Better Speech,* by Louise Abney and Dorothy Miniace, there are some simple rhymes, offered for practice in the enunciation of letter sounds. They may also be used as a first step in group speaking. The rhymes in this chapter are quoted from that text, and suggestions for part division are offered.

If copies of the text are not available, so that children may read the following rhyme from the book, it should be written on the board and then read and discussed by the group. The point that the voice of each animal is different from the others should be brought out.

GETTING-UP TIME

Group I { "Bow-wow," said the pup,
           "It is time to get up."

Group II { "Coo-coo," said the dove,
            From the roof high above.

Group III { "Moo-moo," said the cow,
             "I am getting up now."

Group IV { "Caw, caw," called the crow,
            "What makes you so slow?"

When the children have enjoyed the rhyme and caught its spirit, the suggestion for group speaking may be made. As indicated, the rhyme divides readily into four parts. Perhaps, as a beginning, children may be allowed to choose the animal about which they are to read. Whatever plan is followed, the class should be divided into four groups about equal in number, and a couplet should be assigned to each group.

Before attempting the group reading, emphasis should be placed upon (a) proper timing, (b) suiting the voice to the animal's voice and manner of giving his call, (c) making the group voice sound as one voice, and (d) silent groups listening to the speaking groups.

A successful outcome will probably lead to the repetition of the group speaking of "Getting-Up Time" each morning for a few days. At each rendition, the groups should interchange parts so that all have an opportunity to adjust their voices to the calls of the different creatures. In general, memorization of stanzas or poems is not necessary; yet with such simple rhymes as are given in this chapter, children will soon learn the lines without special effort.

A pleasant, alert, and interested conversational tone is required in the poem "Snowflakes." The difficulty will lie in speaking as a single voice. To attain this end, rhythm and rhyme must be sensed by the group.

SNOWFLAKES

Group I
{ The snowflakes are falling
  By ones and by twos.

Group II
{ There is snow on my jacket
  And snow on my shoes;

Group III
{ There is snow on the bushes
  And snow on the trees,

All
{ It's snowing on everything
  Now, if you please.

Before attempting group speaking, develop the mood of the rhyme. Read the stanzas to the group. Then ask, "How do you feel when you see the first snow? Are you excited? surprised? happy? Do you like to have snowflakes on your cap and coat? Do you like to see snow on the bushes and trees?" Let individual children try the stanzas for Groups I, II, and III, letting each suggest the tone of voice that he thinks will best express his feeling at seeing the snow begin to fall. Should it be a sad tone or a glad tone? Should the tone show surprise as well as pleasure?

When the mood has been established, groups may be selected and group speaking attempted.

After a first reading of "The Nursery Clock," there should be discussion along the lines suggested by the following questions:

> Where does the clock hang?
> Is it about the size of our schoolroom clock?
> How loudly do you think it ticks?
> Who can make the "tick-tock" sound like the clock's voice?

When the correct sound is established, when all lines and words in the rhyme are familiarized, and when the rhyme and rhythm are sensed, it is time to divide into groups. This poem is a good one for utilizing the refrain technique, where the teacher repeats the poem, and the children say "tick-tock" together. Another plan is to have the "tick-tock" come from different parts of the room. For this arrangement, there should be a "tick-tock" group of several voices for each stanza of the rhyme, the remainder of the class speaking the main lines.

THE NURSERY CLOCK

Main Group	The nursery clock hangs high on the wall,
3 or 4 Voices	Tick-tock, tick-tock;
Main Group	And every morning I hear its voice call—
3 or 4 Voices	Tick, tick, tock!
Main Group	High on the wall it is running all day,
3 or 4 Voices	Tick-tock, tick-tock;
Main Group	Ticking the seconds and minutes away—
3 or 4 Voices	Tick, tick, tock!
Main Group	Each morning it hustles me out of my bed,
3 or 4 Voices	Tick-tock, tick-tock;
Main Group	At evening it's ticking while prayers are said—
3 or 4 Voices	Tick, tick, tock!

The rhyme "Hippety Hippety Hop" is a great favorite with young children. If the rhyme is written on the board, it should first be read aloud to the children. Perhaps two children will be eager to play the story told by the poem, one taking the part of white bunny and the other the part of black bunny. The following arrangement combines antiphonal and refrain techniques.

HIPPETY HIPPETY HOP

Group I	A little white bunny Went out to play—
Small Group	Hippety, hippety, hop;
Group II	A little black bunny Came down the way—
Small Group	Hippety, hippety, hop.
Groups I and II	The two little bunnies Had fun that day—
Small Group	Hippety, hippety, hop;
Groups I and II	They spoke to each other In the very best way—
Small Group	Hippety, hippety, hop.
Group II	The little black bunny Then turned to say—
Small Group	Hippety, hippety, hop.
Group II	"I'd like to play, but I cannot stay. Let's meet again some other day—"
Small Group	Hippety, hippety, hop!

The very light tripping of the bunnies on their padded feet should be emphasized. The idea that the voice can bring out this lightness in saying "hippety, hippety, hop" can be developed.

After such development of the feeling for the rhyme, the groups may be selected and the rhyme read.

Finding Appropriate Poems The teacher will find suitable poems in any anthology of children's poetry. Many school readers offer some poems, and perhaps one or more of them may be adapted to choral speaking. For the early, more mechanical stage, such as is exemplified by the rhyme "Getting-Up Time," some of the other nursery rhymes may be used.

For a later stage, in which children are able to sense the mood of the lines, suitable poems may be found in any of the anthologies listed at the close of Chapter 3. Criteria for selection should be: (*a*) brevity, (*b*) simplicity of vocabulary and phrasing, (*c*) marked rhythm, (*d*) appeal to children in thought and structure, (*e*) contrast of ideas, (*f*) literary quality.

Ends to Be Sought In any work with choral speaking, the ends to be sought are:

1 Complete enjoyment on the part of the group
2 Literary appreciation (sensing mood, thought, and picturization)
3 Development of a sense of rhythm and phrasing
4 Ear training through rhyme and rhythm
5 Clear enunciation and correct pronunciation
6 Flexibility in volume, quality, and tone of voice
7 Perfect rapport of the group

Above all, choral speaking should not be used as a show feature. It is not primarily intended as a performance before an audience.

With young children, its major purposes lie in meeting the ends enumerated on page 105. Special stress should be placed upon group enjoyment. Choral speaking is an ancient folk art, and it was originally performed solely for the pleasure of the performing group. This ancient conception should persist with respect to choral speaking with young children in the classroom.

Bibliography

TEXT FOR YOUNG CHILDREN

ABNEY, LOUISE, and MINIACE, DOROTHY. *This Way to Better Speech.* World Book Company, Yonkers-on-Hudson, New York

A speech reader addressed to the child. Offers a complete course in phonetic sounds of letters. Includes rhymes and jingles for speech correction and improvement. Content and vocabulary on second-grade level. Provides for a beginning in choral speaking.

CHORAL SPEAKING

ABNEY, LOUISE, and ROWE, GRACE. *Choral Speaking Arrangements for the Lower Grades.* Expression Company, Magnolia, Massachusetts

ARBUTHNOT, MAY HILL. *Children and Books,* Chapter 9. Scott, Foresman and Company, Chicago 11

DE WITT, MARGUERITE E., and Others. *Practical Methods in Choral Speaking.* Expression Company

GULLAN, MARJORIE. *Choral Speaking.* Expression Company

SCOTT, LOUISE and THOMPSON, J. J. *Talking Time.* Webster Publishing Company, St. Louis 3

SWANN, MONA. *An Approach to Choral Speech.* Expression Company

GENERAL

See Bibliography for Chapter 1.

5 | *Written Expression*

At the stage of development when six-year-old children may have achieved a reasonable degree of ease and effectiveness in the use of oral language, it is altogether likely that they will have little or no ability to express their ideas in writing. They may have a speaking vocabulary of several thousand words; they may enunciate and articulate words quite clearly and correctly; their sentences, while simple in structure and quite short, may be simple or compound or complex. As for writing, they may have learned at home or in kindergarten to print their own names. But they will have had little occasion for, or experience in, expressing their ideas in writing until after they enter first grade.

Occasions for oral communication in the first grade present themselves constantly; therefore, oral language activities receive major stress. However, the children do have real need for written records from time to time. For example, in planning their school garden, the second-grade children in one school kept the following records, some of them written on the board and some posted on the bulletin board: a list of tools needed, a list of seeds to buy, a chart of jobs to be done in the garden, workers on a committee to do each job, and a diary telling day-to-day progress in planting and cultivating the garden. In the first grade, the teacher would have done the writing for the class; but these second-grade children had mastered manuscript writing and could go far toward keeping records and recording their ideas independently. By consulting their word boxes (described later in the chapter under "Spelling"), they could manage most of the spelling, which was their chief handicap in independent writing in the first grade. The slower learners in the group continued to copy the labels and the records that were dictated to the teacher, though all of them did some simple independent writing.

Many children enter the second grade with quite limited ability to write independently, owing to the following handicaps: their sentence sense is inadequate; they have not yet established habits of using capital letters and punctuation marks correctly; they can spell but a few words; they find the physical act of writing so laborious that they must concentrate upon the making of letters to the exclusion of thought about what they wish to say; and they have not yet learned to organize ideas for expression.

From the beginning of the year, therefore, the second-grade teacher must give definite attention to each of these factors that contribute to the total act of expressing oneself in writing. She must discover at once in what respect her group is weak along these lines, and devise a specific and well-planned program for: (*a*) developing sentence sense; (*b*) habituating the correct uses of capital letters and punctuation marks; (*c*) improving ability to spell and thus increasing the writing vocabulary; and (*d*) improving handwriting and developing ease in writing.

Developing Sentence Sense

A child begins to express himself in sentences in his early years, before he enters school, and his spoken sentences express complete thoughts. But he acquires this ability quite unconsciously,

Setting up a classroom post office is often an outgrowth of children's interest in making valentines, an activity shown in the opening illustration of this chapter. Devising and writing appropriate valentine greetings (or of Christmas or birthday greetings as the case might be), as well as addressing envelopes, call for the exercise of writing skills such as uses of capital letters and correct spelling. Setting up the post office motivates other expressional activities such as discussion, listing plans, and listing names of committee members.

for he develops it entirely by imitation of those about him. Nevertheless, he does express himself orally (tells what he wishes to say, or asks a question) in complete sentences.

Stress on the Sentence in Reading In the first grade he hears the word *sentence* used frequently. As he learns to read, his teacher will say, "Who can read the first *sentence?*" or "Which *sentence* tells you the puppy's name?" Thus the child grows in the knowledge (unconsciously, of course) that a sentence may tell something or ask something. He even learns how sentences are set apart, in print or in writing, for he sees that there is a capital letter to tell him where a sentence begins, and that there is some kind of mark to show him the end of the sentence. Otherwise he could not read from his reader, or read the group story that the teacher has written on the board or on a chart. When she writes on the board, the teacher will strengthen the pupils' concept of sentence form by occasionally calling their attention to the capital letter with which she begins the first word in each sentence of the story they dictate; also, to the period or question mark that she places at the end of a sentence. Thus the teacher helps the children to understand the mechanics of the written or printed sentence.

In the second grade the teacher will work along these same lines. Questions like the following may be injected without interfering with interest in reading:

> "Here is a new story. The first *sentence* tells where Toni went. Who can read that *sentence?* Which *sentence* tells what Toni found?"

> "John, the next *sentence* is a short one. Will you read it to us?"

> "Mary, will you read the *long sentence* that comes next?"

"You have just learned the word *elephant.* Can you
find two sentences on the next page that have the word
elephant in them?"

Again, in composing a class story, the teacher will ask, "What
shall we tell in our *first sentence?*" "Who can suggest the *second
sentence?*" and so on. When the story is completed, she may ask,
"Isn't this a good, long story? How many sentences did we put
in it? How can you tell?"

Building the Sentence Concept   There is no formal sentence
work in the second grade. If, by the end of the year, the child
senses the fact that a sentence tells something, or asks a question,
or tells what to do (as in directions or rules), he has grasped the
concept of the complete thought.

In both oral and written work, the teacher should strive to
eliminate the fault of stringing sentences together with "and,"
"and-a," "why-a," "so-a," or "then-a." As this fault is eliminated
in oral expression, the sentence concept is strengthened, and improvement of the written sentence follows.

In connection with oral stories, such as telling news items to
the class, the teacher may ask, "Could you tell where Danny's
sentences ended? Did that help you to understand him better?"
Again, in connection with a planned story, she may suggest,
"When you tell your story, stop and think what you wish to say
before you begin each sentence. That will help you to make a
better sentence, and it will help us to catch up with what you are
telling us."

Corrective Work   During a period of spontaneous expression,
it is not advisable to correct a child who is guilty of the *and*-fault
lest he be discouraged from volunteering to speak. Above all, no
child should be repressed or be forced into self-consciousness in

his early desires or efforts to speak. The error should be brought up in a period devoted to technical phases of expression—not in a period in which voluntary, spontaneous expression is the major goal.

During a period devoted to corrective teaching, the teacher may say, "I heard someone tell a story in this way . . ." and write on the board a three-sentence story having sentences connected by *and*'s. "Can you tell how many sentences there are? Why not? Read the story silently. (*Pause.*) What do you think the first sentence is, Julie? Do we need this *and*? (*Crosses it out.*)

"What is the second sentence? Do we need this *and*? (*Crosses it out.*)

"Now read the first sentence again, Tommy. What do we need to place at the end? (*Places the period.*) Where else do we need a period? (*Places it.*)

"What do we use to show the beginning of a sentence? Where should we put capital letters?" (*Supplies them.*)

It is to be observed that the "and-a's" and "why-a's" are largely due to slow thinking or to lack of an idea as to what to say next. As children are directed to observe closely, and as they engage in enriching activities and experiences, ideas will multiply and children will speak and write less hesitantly. It is only as children become proficient in speaking in complete sentences that they can write sentences that are not run together.

Capitalization and Punctuation

In the first grade, children should learn to use capital letters for the following: (*a*) their own names, (*b*) names of classmates, (*c*) names of pets, (*d*) the word *I*, (*e*) first word in a sentence. However, since their written work is largely copied from the board, it cannot be assumed that children entering the second

Spring

Spring is here. Jane
likes spring and flowers.
Ann likes birds and flowers.

The Robin

He comes in Spring.
His breast is red.
We like robins.

Bobby

Observation of spring phenomena gave rise to these stories by first-grade children, one a group story and the other written independently.

grade will have learned to use capital letters in these instances independently or automatically. It is likely that the second-grade teacher will need to do some reteaching.

The first use of capital letters in the second grade will probably occur in connection with heading papers. The group should be taught at once the prescribed heading for use in the school and grade, and should understand that the heading is to be used for each written lesson. If, in addition to the child's own name (first and last), the date and the name of the school are used in the heading, the use of capital letters for the name of the month and of the school can thus be established and habituated in connection with a very practical daily need. In a special place on the board, the teacher should write the name of the school (calling attention to capital letters and to spelling), and also the date, changing the latter from day to day and month to month. It may be advisable to reserve the writing of the date until the latter part of the year.

In connection with a co-operative note, which the teacher writes on the board, the use of capital letters in the greeting and in the closing will be noted. However, children need only be instructed to copy these capital letters correctly, since they will seldom be expected to write a note independently in the first or second grade. Each child should also learn how to write his own address, using capital letters correctly for street, town or county, and state. But general rules for the use of capital letters should not be taught.

From time to time, written stories, notes, and notices may call for the writing of other proper names. The use of capital letters in such instances should be pointed out. Yet the general principle of teaching the use of capital letters only in connection with day-to-day practical situations should apply, as rules mean nothing to young children.

In the early grades the uses of punctuation marks are few, including the period and question mark for sentence endings and perhaps the period to follow *Mr.* and *Mrs.* These should be habituated by constant use. If the comma after the greeting of a letter, in a date, and between city and state are needed, they will usually be copied from the board.

Spelling

As children progress in their developmental reading program, they learn the various skills of word recognition. Among these skills are the names of the letters of the alphabet and also their sounds, taken singly or in digraphs (blends). They also learn how to analyze a word with respect to its parts, such as (*a*) syllables; (*b*) *s* or *es* endings; (*c*) *ing* and *d* or *ed* endings; (*d*) parts of a compound word; and (*e*) finding little words in big words. These same skills carry over into the ability to attack the spelling of a word. Children, therefore, gradually acquire readiness for spelling instruction as they learn to attack new words in their reading vocabulary independently.

Actually, most children do learn to spell, without conscious effort, the words that they commonly use. They watch the teacher as she writes their news stories and experience stories on the board. They engage in matching exercises in which they must closely inspect word and phrase cards in order to find the corresponding word or phrase in a chart story. They learn to copy announcements and records that the teacher has written down for them. They do seatwork in connection with the development of reading skills in which they write certain words frequently. As a result, such common words as *jump, come, school, home,* and *mother* are learned incidentally—perhaps not through studying them letter by letter, but by configuration; that is, by retaining a picture of the total word instead of thinking of the component letters. At any rate, many first-grade children can write independently as many as 50 to 100 words by the end of the school year; and in the second-grade they continue to learn many words through incidental means.

Even in situations in which the second-grade program includes regular spelling lessons based on a locally prescribed list or on

Dear Mother,
    There will be no school next Friday. All the teachers are going to a meeting.
           Your son,
           Harry

The alert teacher seizes every opportunity to provide for written expression in various forms. Here a special school occasion was used to motivate the writing of a letter to a parent. The letter was first planned and dictated by the group and later copied by each child.

a textbook, the chances are that, with the help of the teacher, second-grade children will also have their own list of words selected on the basis of current writing needs. One effective procedure is for each child to have a sturdy cardboard word box about a foot long and five inches wide. In it should be 26 stiff guide cards, each with a letter of the alphabet on a projection at the top. Then, as a useful word that a pupil wishes to master is met, the child can write the word on a piece of paper and file it alphabetically. Thereafter he may consult his word box for any word he has placed there.

Teachers who are trying to determine a local list will do well to consult graded lists such as those presented by Fitzgerald or Hildreth. (See Bibliography at the end of this chapter.) Any word of current need that seems too hard or that the children do not need to master at the present time may be listed temporarily on the board or on a chart so that the children may copy the word when they need to write it. For those words that are likely to be generally useful, spelling lessons may be planned.

When a prescribed spelling text is used, perhaps the best procedure is to consult the summary list that most spellers and spelling workbooks offer for review at the end of the book. From this list may be selected the words for which the pupils have immediate and frequent need. A check mark may be placed before each word that is selected and taught. Thus much of the year's spelling list may be covered. An individual pupil may also have a list of words that he compiles on the basis of his personal needs.

Children should, in general, learn the spelling of such words as they need to use frequently in their writing. From among the new words learned in connection with a group experience or current interest, the teacher and the children should select those key words that may be needed to use in writing a picture legend, a label, a notice, or a story. These words should be written on a chart and kept for the duration of the activity or interest so that the children may consult the list as need arises. For example, while interest persists in the trip to the train mentioned earlier in this book, the following words may be listed:

trip	sidetrack	steam	conductor
train	dining car	engine	porter
ready	sleeper	engineer	passenger

By no means should the children be expected to master the spelling of these words. Yet such a reference list instills in the child the idea that *there is a correct way to spell any word,* and it sets up the habit of finding out the correct spelling when he does not know it. The child should also be encouraged to ask the teacher for a correct spelling when he is doing original writing.

Handwriting

Skill in handwriting will condition the effectiveness of a child's written expression. Therefore handwriting is a factor in the language program. It is not the function of this book to prescribe the procedures for the teaching of writing. Each system of writing instruction gives specific directions for teaching manuscript or cursive writing. It is necessary, however, for the teacher to recognize the fact that as long as a child must be completely absorbed in his efforts to write—must concentrate on what his fingers are doing—he cannot concentrate on the ideas he has set out to express. When a child omits words from his sentences, when he omits letters from words that he really knows how to spell, when his sentences are barren and but vaguely connected in thought, then the teacher must consider whether having to make a tremendous effort to write is at least one source of his trouble. It is worth the time and effort to give extra attention

Sally   Grade 2

My name is Sally Fox.

I am six years old.

Please bring a doll buggy.

I have been a good girl.

The approach of Christmas motivated Sally to write this appeal for a special gift. This is especially good writing and general arrangement for a young child in early second grade.

to that child in the writing period or in special periods for individual instruction.

The teacher must be sure that the regular lessons and exercises in learning manuscript writing forms carry over into normal writing situations. Most lessons in manuscript writing are tied to reading, social studies, or other current classroom activities. The children have thought of a sentence or two that they wish to write. The teacher writes it on the board and the children copy it.

However, certain letters may be difficult to make, and specific practice on such letters may be desirable. Before the close of such a practice lesson in writing, it is well to ask each child to write a

sentence telling something he wishes to say; or to dictate a
sentence for him to write—perhaps a sentence about some interesting class experience of the day; or to let one of the children suggest an interesting sentence to write. Even at the risk of a mis-
spelled word or an omitted period, it is desirable to have the
child's writing effort carry over into the practical situation of
using writing to express thought so that the act of writing may
become almost automatic.

The Teacher as Secretary

For Group Communication Much of the written expression in
the first grade and in the early part of the second grade will be
the co-operative work of the group, in which children suggest
various sentences, the group judges and selects the one that is
preferred, and the teacher writes the accepted sentences on the
board. The daily news story, a report of the latest step in a class
activity that will be part of a longer record of a unit as a whole,
an announcement, a note or letter to mothers about a school
party, various lists (names of pupil helpers, their duties, committee assignments, materials needed for a project)—these constitute
most of the kinds of communication that the children will engage
in. This type of writing activity is described fully in an earlier
chapter.

For the Individual Child The teacher also records ideas for
individual children. On some occasions, articles are brought by
the children for a classroom exhibit, and each contributor may
wish to make his own label. A child decides what he wants to
write on his label, and the teacher writes it on a slip of paper
for him to copy. On another occasion, a child may have drawn a
picture, and may then wish to compose a legend to explain it.

Pony

Pony wants something. Tom said Look Mother Pony wants something. Have you a surprisefor Pony? Mother said Yes, I have a surprise for Pony. It is a big red apple. Pony will like it.

A story written independently by a second-grade pupil. It exemplifies an unusual grasp of sentence sense as well as comprehension of sequential order of ideas.

Again, the teacher writes down what the child dictates so that he may copy his own legend.

After Christmas, each child in one second grade brought his favorite toy to school. The children were later asked if they would like to draw pictures of their toys. The response was enthusiastic, and crayons were immediately in evidence. As the children drew, the teacher moved among them. Inevitably some of them explained their pictures to her. Upon suggestion from the teacher, each child composed a story or legend for his picture. The teacher then wrote on a slip of paper the one or two sentences that the child dictated, and he later copied his story below the picture. At the suggestion of one child, the pictures were eventually made into a *Toyland Book*, which was a favorite in the classroom reading center.

An occasional imaginative child has a desire to make up stories or verse. He may have facility in writing down ideas for himself; but until a child has reached the stage of independent writing, the teacher acts as his secretary whenever he expresses a desire to record his creative production. She reproduces the story or verse on a chart for the group to read. The child then copies it and places it in a class book of stories and verse, or in his own book.

Preparation for Independent Writing

For children who do not develop writing skill with considerable ease, authorities in language instruction recommend definite steps in building up the fundamental skills involved in independent writing. These are: (*a*) copywork, (*b*) studied dictation, (*c*) unstudied dictation, (*d*) the unfinished story, and (*e*) independent writing. If possible, a series of lessons following these steps should be fitted in as part of a larger activity, such as the study of community helpers or of animal friends.

Copywork   Nearly all of the copywork will follow co-operative stories, reports, or notes that were written on a chart or on the board as the children dictated the sentences, one by one. The teaching of the necessary skills of writing precedes such copywork, as suggested earlier. Teacher and children together study the elements of form, such as placement of title, the margins, indention (after true paragraph form is observed), letter form,

Peanuts

Once upon a time there was a big grey elephant named Peanuts.
He went from place to place with the circus.
He liked to do tricks and make the children laugh.
Kenny

An original second-grade story with content derived from a vicarious experience through reading.

capitalization, punctuation, the sentence, and the spelling of un-familiar words. The children are instructed to copy by phrases rather than by the single word, or by spelling out single words in a laborious way. The standard for all copywork is *perfection*—one hundred per cent accuracy. Almost without exception, chil-dren will at first copy what the "teacher-secretary" has written for them. However, very bright children will soon develop con-siderable independence; but slower-learning pupils will profit from lessons in studied dictation which are described below.

Studied Dictation   After copywork has familiarized the group with manuscript form and with the common uses of capitaliza-tion and punctuation, the slow-learning children in mid-second grade will profit from lessons in studied dictation. The sentences, the note, the notice, or the story to be dictated should be studied under teacher direction. The teacher should list the words that children have not learned to spell, writing them on the board in the order of their appearance so that each word can be easily located by a child who needs to refer to the list. The teacher's dictation should follow a very specific technique, the steps being:

1   Read the entire selection (now concealed) while the children listen to recall the sentences in it.
2   Read the first sentence so that the children can visualize it and recall the capitalization and end punctuation.
3   Read the first thought phrase in the sentence (two to five words) while the children listen closely.
4   Have the children repeat the phrase that has just been read to offset their naturally short span of attention.
5   Have them write what they have just repeated, looking at the board for the spelling of any difficult word.
6   Read the next phrase in the first sentence, have the chil-dren repeat it, and then write it.

7 Repeat steps 2-6 for each phrase within the sentence.

8 Follow steps 2-7 with each sentence.

As in copywork, the standard for dictation work is perfection, or as near one hundred per cent accuracy as possible. Each paper should be inspected by the teacher. Errors should be pointed out and discussed with each child, who then corrects them. By this procedure, children who do not easily master the mechanics of writing soon make real progress toward independent mastery of spelling, capitalization, and punctuation.

Unstudied Dictation Some children soon become proficient in studied dictation, while others need much practice. The former group should proceed to unstudied dictation as soon as they are ready for it, not wait for their slower-learning classmates.

In unstudied dictation, the teacher writes a co-operative story on paper. The children do not see the story before they write. However, the teacher lists on the board, in the order of occurrence, any words whose spelling might prove troublesome. She should ask questions on items of form that will appear in the exercise, such as, "How do you write the name of a pet?" "How do you write the first word in a sentence?" In dictating, she should follow all the steps that are listed on pages 124-125, as the children need this very detailed guidance for writing stories they have not previously read, discussed, and studied as to form.

The Unfinished Story In an unfinished story, the beginning of a simple story is copied from the board or from a chart, or written from dictation. The teacher then suggests that the children imagine how the story might end and write the ending in their own words. The story should be of such character that the outcome may readily be sensed and may be expressed in one or two sentences. Specimens of unfinished stories follow.

The teacher begins in this manner: "Here is part of a story. Let's read it. Then you must think what happened next." After skillful questioning, the teacher suggests that each child finish the story as he thinks it might end.

A Happy Surprise

David wanted a new pet.
His black and white puppy had run away.
It never came back.
One morning David heard a sound outside the door.
It was a soft little sound.
—?―――――――――――――――――――――――――
—?―――――――――――――――――――――――――

Fun at Home

Would Saturday never come?
Dennis and Rickie could hardly wait.
They were going on a picnic in the park.
But it was raining Saturday!
Then Mother planned a nice surprise.
—?―――――――――――――――――――――
—?―――――――――――――――――――――

Some children in the latter half of the first grade and most children in the second grade should learn to write their stories in paragraph form. The first stories should therefore be simple and easy to write, as is the sample unfinished story that follows.

Feeding the Babies

Mrs. Robin was busy. She was finding worms. She fed them to her babies. One baby was too greedy.

At the close of the writing period, the children enjoy reading their stories to one another.

Time for School.
"Run. Tom", said Mother.
"Run, Betty, run.
It is time to go to school.
Run fast." Away ran
Tom and Betty.
"Good-by, Mother," they
called. "We are on our
way to school. Good-by
Flip."

A story written independently by a second-grade child. The use of quotation marks is exceptional, and probably developed from the child's personal observation of their use in stories that he has read in books.

Independent Writing As soon as the more proficient children demonstrate ability to write down their own ideas, they should be permitted to do so. Naturally there will be some words that they cannot spell. Some suggestions for handling this situation are given here:

(1) The children may be asked to think through their proposed stories and decide on the words they wish to use. Individuals may then ask for help with words they cannot spell. These the teacher will list on the board.

(2) Each child may proceed with his writing. When a child wishes to use a word that he cannot spell, he may leave a blank space and proceed. When the teacher has time to help him, he may ask for the spelling of the word. If it is a common and useful word, he may copy it on a word strip to file in his word box.

(3) The child may have a sheet of paper lying on his desk. He may try out the spelling of words that are troublesome. The word that "looks right" may be written in the story; or, at least, the probable beginning letters may be recorded in the story, and the child may ask the teacher for the correct spelling later.

(4) When there are unfamiliar words that the child is likely to use often, he may (and should) begin an alphabetical list, or use his alphabetized word box. Another plan would be to make his own dictionary. The pages of a notebook may be lettered successively *A*, *B*, *C*, and so on through the alphabet. All words beginning with *a* can be written on the *A* page, the *b* words on the *B* page, and so on.

(5) Possibly the most important practice for the child to follow is for him to hold himself responsible for looking up the spelling of words he needs to use. He may consult his reader, library book (if he is writing about a character or happening in it), or one of the picture dictionaries on the shelf of his classroom.

Standards of Attainment By the end of the second grade, all the children should have gained some degree of ability to write independently, though all children may not have attained the same standard as to quality of content. In their independent writing, however, they should have established the following habits as to manuscript form and as to the mechanics of writing:

1 Place the correct heading at the top of the page in the right position, capitalizing correctly.
2 Keep a fairly even left margin about an inch wide.
3 Begin the first word in each sentence with a capital letter.
4 Capitalize the word *I*.
5 Place a period at the end of a statement.
6 Place a question mark at the end of a question.
7 Use capital letters for names of persons and pets.

Children should also be habitually neat in their written work and careful of their spelling. If the paragraph form is taught, indention will become almost habitual.

Bibliography

See Bibliography for Chapter 1, especially those entries on communication of ideas and selected chapters in the general references.

SPELLING

FITZGERALD, JAMES A. *A Basic Life Spelling Vocabulary*. The Bruce Publishing Company, Milwaukee 1, Wisconsin

HILDRETH, GERTRUDE H. *Teaching Spelling*. Henry Holt and Company, Inc., New York 17

As compared with fluency and spontaneity of expression growing out of wide interests and rich social experiences, correct word usage is not necessarily of first importance in the first and second grades. That the children have ideas to express and that they have a desire to express them interestingly and effectively are the more important ends to be sought in the promotion of the language arts program in these grades.

A teacher can, however, help her children to develop habits of correct speech and to eliminate incorrect usage without impairing spontaneity or destroying the social values of communication. There are a few gross errors in word usage that she should strive to eliminate; and she should also strive for simple speech correction.

Investigations in the field of language have demonstrated that few errors in speech and in word usage are common to an entire group. Errors are highly individualized, and the teacher will have to plan much small-group and individual instruction.

Survey of Group Habits of Word Usage

A prerequisite of such planning is a careful survey of the usage habits of the group. It will be discovered that some children make almost no errors of the flagrant type, thus reflecting a home environment in which they hear fairly good language. There is the possibility, however, that most of the children will enunciate a few sounds improperly or use some grossly incorrect word forms common to the community. When this is the case, the teacher should list those errors for stress.

In general, the survey becomes a task of observing individual habits of expression as children talk spontaneously. Probably not all errors made by the children can be eliminated, but a few should be listed for special stress. The following lists suggest those errors from which the teacher may select.

I. Speech faults
 A. Baby talk
 B. Lisping
 C. Faulty sounding of **l, sh, s, r, z, th,** and **wh**

II. Word usage

 A. Forms that are not words, or are mispronunciation; as,

"ain't"	"growed"	"theirn"
"hain't"	"knowed"	"yourn"
"brung"	"hisn"	"youse"
"clumb"	"ourn"	"hisself"
"bust"	"hern"	"theirselves"

B. The impolite habit of mentioning oneself first; as,
"I and Father" went.   Please help "me and Jim."

C. Incorrect use of pronoun in such expressions as "Mary and me are ready," and "Joe helped Tim and I."

D. Some flagrant errors with verbs in frequent use; as,
"I done it."   "He come late yesterday."
"I seen it."   "I run home last night."
"He has went."

E. Incorrect expressions, such as "them books," or "this here clay," or "that there picture."

Part I above is especially important in the first grade, whereas attention to items in Part II should be handled incidentally and individually. Because children vary so greatly with respect to the speech faults listed in Part I, it is usually necessary to deal with individual children in trying to eliminate them. No teacher should attempt to work on all the errors listed. The attempt to work on many errors is wasteful.

The Program in Speech

The teaching of speech is a very important phase of the language program. While the specialist in speech is the only one qualified to treat a really serious speech defect in the occasional child, the classroom teacher can do much to improve the more or less faulty speech of all children in the group. The program in speech should be directed toward (*a*) voice quality, (*b*) enunciation, (*c*) pronunciation, and (*d*) expression or intonation to convey meaning.

A Planned and Consistent Program In general, children in the first and second grades need a planned and consistent course of training in speech. They still retain many of the careless habits of speech picked up (through imitation) in the preschool years. In fact, in many homes parents and older children actually enjoy the "baby talk" and the incorrect pronunciation of letter sounds in the speech of the younger child in the home, and they thus promote their persistence into the school years.

Some of these irregularities of speech are due to incorrect use of the organs of speech, some to immaturity, some to faulty hearing, some to lack of attentive listening, and some to mere ignorance of correct letter sounds. The program of speech correction must therefore be directed along several lines.

Since instruction in speech is such an important aspect of the language arts program, affecting both reading and expression, many second-grade teachers find it necessary to have a set of supplementary speech readers for use by the children who need correction. The use of a text of this type assures the teacher that she is promoting a logical and consistent—in truth, a correct—program for the improvement of speech within her group.

Voice Quality Children are unconscious imitators of adults— a fact that sometimes leads to desirable and often to undesirable practices on the part of children. It is therefore important that the teacher's voice and speech be such that desirable results will follow from the tendency of her group to imitate her.

The teacher's voice should be well-rounded (not thin), moderately pitched (especially not too high), of moderate volume (not loud), melodious or well-modulated (not flat or monotonous), pleasing (not harsh or shrill), and lively (not drawling or languid). Children who work with a teacher having a pleasing, well-modulated voice and a stimulating, alert, interested manner of speaking are likely to speak in similar tones. If the teacher enunciates distinctly so that she need not raise her voice to make it possible for children to hear and understand her words, the children unconsciously acquire similar clarity of enunciation. Children may be helped to acquire flexible, expressive voices if they have many opportunities to repeat verse with contrasting ideas and to read aloud conversation that reflects varying emotions such as surprise, joy, and fear. Choral reading is also an aid to voice improvement.

Structural characteristics of the vocal chambers largely determine the fundamental tonal qualities of the voice. However, a high-pitched, nasal, or monotonous voice is often imitative or merely a matter of habit; it can, therefore, be changed through intelligent training. A few pupils may need individual attention if their voice-placement is far back in the throat, too high in the head, or forward in the nasal passages.

Enunciation   Young children often speak indistinctly because they do not use their lips, teeth (or jaws), and tongue actively. The teacher may sometimes demonstrate the use of these organs of speech by pronouncing some vowels and consonants with somewhat exaggerated use of lips, teeth, and tongue.

Demonstrations might well proceed in the following order. While lips, teeth, and tongue perform a function in making all letter sounds, there are certain consonants that use one or the other conspicuously, as indicated:

Lips: **b f m q v w y**
Teeth (Jaws): **c d f g h j k s t v z**
Tongue: **d l n s x z**

Pronouncing words beginning and ending with these consonants will afford further practice in using lips, teeth, and tongue. Pairs of words like the following may be written on a chart or the board, pronounced by the teacher with emphasis on beginning and ending sounds and with slightly exaggerated movement of lips, jaws, and tongue, and then repeated by the children:

bat — rub	me — am	kite — lick
funny — gruff	want — now	like — will
do — red	to — not	nice — soon

Internal consonant sounds should be enunciated as in:

rubber	sudden	gully	wither	matter
ribbon	hidden	silly	mother	bitter
labor	rider	gaily	father	later

In pronouncing such words, the children may well exaggerate the use of lips, teeth, and tongue in producing beginning, internal, and final consonant sounds. The exaggeration provides a kind of exercise for limbering up the muscles of lips, tongue, and jaw and making them more flexible and active. Such demonstration and practice will be sufficient for the majority of the group. The "lazy" speaker—a child who enunciates letters or words with scarcely a visible movement of lips, teeth, and tongue—will need intensive individual training in the enunciation of consonants.

Attention should also be given to the placement of vowel sounds. The child can readily feel that these sounds arise from the back of the mouth cavity, though the different vowel sounds and the different sounds of a single vowel will require different manipulation of teeth and lips. The following more common sounds of each vowel should be demonstrated by the teacher to show clearly how the sound is placed:

ā (āble)	ē (ēven)	ī (īce)	ō (ōld)	ū (ūse)
ă (ăt)	ĕ (ĕnd)	ĭ (ĭt)	ŏ (ŏdd)	ŭ (ŭp)
ä (ärm)				

The diacritical markings need not be taught. It is better to list words like the following for the children to read and pronounce:

Sounds of a			*Sounds of e*	
able	at	arm	even	end
ate	am	art	feel	echo
take	fan	farm	beet	leg

Sounds of i		*Sounds of o*		*Sounds of u*	
ice	it	old	odd	use	up
nice	tin	over	ox	June	uncle
fine	sink	cold	fox	music	sun

The main stress in the work with enunciation, however, will have to do with the pronunciation of words in sentences. Nonsense sentences containing a number of words beginning or ending with the same marked letter sounds are also helpful with "lazy" speakers. Sentences like the following may be written on the board and used for oral practice:

1 Fred found four fine files.
2 Tell Tony to take two turns.
3 Let Scott put that cat out.

The teacher may also make good use of nursery rhymes. Following are titles of rhymes that feature sounds that the children may need to practice:

d Deedle, deedle, dumpling

s See-saw, Margery Daw

w Wee Willie Winkie

m One misty, moisty morning

p Peter, Peter, pumpkin eater

Further attention to the enunciation of words in normal sentences will be a part of the regular reading lesson.

Pronunciation The general practice described under *Enunciation* may not take care of the mispronunciation of certain letters that persists with individual children. The teacher may easily detect such children in the ordinary work in reading. There may be an occasional child who cannot produce correctly the sound of *r*, or *l*, or *w*. Such a child needs individual instruction as to the correct sound of the letter and as to the correct placement and use of speech organs to produce the correct letter sound.

Some young children have difficulty in pronouncing consonant digraphs such as *br, cr, dr, fr, gr, pr, tr*, and *wr; sw* and *tw; bl, cl, pl* and *sl; wh* and *th*. These children may require special instruction and practice along the lines suggested for remedial work with individual letter sounds.

The mispronunciation of certain consonant combinations may be due to a failure to sense letter values, or to the careless disregard of the sound value of one letter. Among such combinations are initial *wh* and final *ng*. Instruction and practice with lists of words like the following are helpful in correcting these faults:

	wh			**ng**
white	when	whale	ring	doing
while	what	whip	sing	being
where	why	whack	bring	flying
which	wheat	whine	wing	going

Such catch-sayings as "Always make *ing* rhyme with *ring*" and "Start to whistle when you say *white*" are helpful reminders.

Other initial combinations that may need attention are *ch, sh*, and *th* (both sounds). Final combinations *sh, th, tch*, and *est* may also need stress. Nonsense sentences embodying such letter combinations are also helpful.

The teacher should watch for other mispronunciations common among her children and list them for correction as a phase of her speech program. Some of the more frequent errors are with the following words:

wish (not "woosh" or "wisht")	help (not "hep")
wash (not "warsh")	ask (not "ast")
any (not "inny")	hold (not "holt")
men (not "min")	heard (not "heerd")
best (not "bes")	burst (not "bust")

The child who mispronounces such words should not be made self-conscious by untactful correction. A group or an individual needing special attention should be taken aside while the rest of the children are otherwise engaged and given special corrective instruction.

It is always best to conduct the speech lessons apart from those periods in which spontaneous oral expression is the goal. During a period of the latter type, the teacher may unobtrusively observe speech needs on the part of the individual and the group and make them the basis of special speech lessons. The use of a supplementary speech text is one good means of keeping speech instruction apart from other oral-expression periods.

Voice Modulation Training in modulation of the voice to bring out the meaning of words and phrases within a sentence, and also of the sentence as a whole, is best handled in the reading period. All good teachers of reading now realize that "word calling" is not reading. Children are reminded to "read the sentence as you would say it yourself" or "read it as you think Betty said it."

Children's spontaneous speech is seldom monotonous or singsong. In fact, from babyhood a child will generally make his tone of voice and verbal intonations reflect his emotion and his meaning. It is only when the child is taken out of the atmosphere of

The making of a bird record is the outcome of the observation tour reflected in the illustration at the opening of this chapter. The use of capital letters for the names of months and days, as well as the study of a current calendar to see how the names of days are abbreviated, are prerequisites of the making of such a record. Such technicalities are better taught from observation than by much emphasis on rules. Reporting when a bird is first seen calls for oral expression. Setting up the record chart calls for orderly thinking and recording. Writing the names of birds calls for correct spelling.

spontaneity that he will think of speech as formal or as a lesson and will therefore utter his words and sentences in a monotonous and lifeless manner. When the language periods are characterized by a freedom and a social atmosphere that invite spontaneous expression, children are likely to speak with expression. Similarly, when the reading period is a period of pleasurable experience during which the child enjoys the thought of what he reads and senses it as the interesting expression of others (rather than a testing period in which the teacher seeks to discover how many words he knows), the child will generally read with expression.

Dramatic reading is one type of exercise calling for special emphasis on expression. For such reading, the teacher asks different children to take the parts of the various characters in the story, and she herself (or other children) reads the parts that carry the story continuity. When children read the parts of the characters, they are advised to "show how the person felt" and to "say it as you think Bob must have said it," thus attaining the desired end of reading with expression.

Dramatization of favorite stories, in which the children recall the dialogue or compose their own speeches, is another means of developing the habit of showing meaning and emotion through the use of the voice. If some children are slow in developing the desired ability in expression, either through timidity or through lack of imagination, their tendency to imitate the expression of their abler classmates will in time override their deficiencies if there is plenty of spontaneous dramatization.

Listening to Oral Reading　Listening to stories and poems read by the teacher is another influence toward the improvement of expression—provided, of course, that *the teacher herself reads well*. A teacher who wishes to bring to her group the fullest enjoyment of literature, as well as the concomitant value of improvement of voice and expression, must school herself in reading aloud until voice, enunciation, pronunciation, and expression all serve to lift the standard and increase the ability of her group along these various lines.

Chapter 3 of this book discusses at length the function of the teacher in reading and telling stories and in reading poems. The bibliography at the close of that chapter lists books on the art of storytelling, as well as anthologies of stories and poems that will serve as sources of appropriate materials for reading aloud. Within the chapter are lists of poems that the teacher may well read aloud.

Methods of Attack on Word Usage

When it is apparent that a given error in word usage persists with an individual or a group, corrective measures should be concentrated upon it. The accepted steps of procedure are:

1 The children look at the correct form on the board or on a chart. (*eye training*)
2 The children listen to the teacher's repetition of the correct form. (*ear training*)
3 They say the form aloud correctly. (*ear* and *speech training*)
4 They read the form correctly in a sentence, or repeat the sentence after the teacher. (*habit forming*)

It is helpful to have the forms for special stress written on charts that may be taken from files and used as needs demand. The following charts were used by one teacher in a campaign against "ain't" and "hain't."

am not	isn't
I am not ready.	Joe isn't here.
I am not late.	Isn't that a robin?
I am not hungry.	Anne isn't coming.
I am not tired.	Isn't it cold today?

aren't	haven't
The books aren't here.	Haven't you a pencil?
Aren't you going?	We haven't voted yet.
You aren't my partner.	Haven't you seen Sue?
Aren't we invited?	I haven't any crayons.

Necessarily, the sentences for such charts should be chosen from among those frequently used by the children, and the words must be selected from the reading vocabulary. Since children learn their speech habits through imitation of forms and expressions that they hear, *ear training* is an important factor in developing habits of correct usage. With any child or any group requiring special practice, the correct method is to place the chart showing correct form before the child, have him read it aloud, and then have him make up sentences using the correct forms. The latter should be inspired by skillful questioning.

The preferred method of instruction in correct usage, then, follows these principles:

1 Individualize the instruction.
2 Concentrate on a very few forms.
3 Present the correct form to eye and ear.
4 Have children repeat the correct form aloud in sentences, some of which are composed by the child.
5 Feature the correct form in many reading charts.

An alert teacher will find frequent opportunities for a few seconds of practice. At the beginning of a drawing period, when all are at attention, she may briefly ask, "*Have you* a red crayon, Jill?" The child should reply, "Yes, *I have* a red crayon" (not "I've got").

In a moment of waiting, the teacher may ask, "Who *ate* the Little Bear's porridge, Joe?" Joe should reply, "Goldilocks *ate* the Little Bear's porridge."

Spirit of Correction Sometimes correction may be given at the time that an error is made, provided that the child is not interrupted in his flow of thought and that he is not embarrassed. For example, Johnny may remark, "Father done the dishes for Mother last night." Upon the conclusion of this remark, the teacher may quietly say, "Your father *did* the dishes. Who *did* them the night before?" in the hope that the child will seize upon the correct form *did* from her own purposeful use of it. If Johnny is a shy child, she may wait until she can speak to him alone. However, if he is a well-adjusted child who can take suggestions without embarrassment, she may suggest at once, "Say 'Father *did* the dishes,' Johnny," in a casual and friendly manner. On the whole, it is preferable that the teacher find frequent occasion to use the correct form of words that the children use improperly. As she does so, the right word will begin to *sound right* to the children and they will begin unconsciously to imitate her.

Language Games

In general, so-called "language games" are not highly successful in habituating correct usage. However, with a few children who are slow to grasp a correct form (which has previously been correctly developed) and who need to hear it repeated frequently, language games may be tried.

The primary considerations in selecting and introducing a game are: (*a*) that the game itself be such that concentration upon *correct usage* is paramount, and (*b*) that the children be ready to center upon *language* as the major interest, rather than upon the physical activity. When lack of interest in a game is apparent, it should be stopped immediately. In any event such a game should not be prolonged more than a few minutes.

The following games are examples of what may be done:

HIDING THE BALL

(To eliminate "has got" and "ain't")

Jack is chosen to leave the room. During his absence, Gladys, the leader, gives a ball to Ralph, who holds his hands behind him, thus hiding the ball. The rest of the children place their hands behind them.

Gladys calls Jack to return to the room. Then she asks, "Jack, who *has* the ball?"

JACK (*looking at Mary*). Is it Mary?

GLADYS. No, it *isn't* Mary.

JACK. Is it Dick?

GLADYS. No, it *isn't* Dick.

JACK. Is it Ralph?

GLADYS. Yes, it is Ralph.

Ralph then leaves the room, and the game proceeds.

TAKE A PEEP

(Practice on *I saw*)

Under a cover on a table or desk, the teacher has concealed a number of small common objects. She then asks, "Anne, will you take a quick peep and tell us one thing that you *saw?*

Anne walks to the table, lifts the cover slightly, and notices one object.

TEACHER. What did you see, Anne?

ANNE. I *saw* a watch.

TEACHER. Bob, take a peep and look for something else.

(*Bob steps forward and looks under the cover.*)

TEACHER. Bob, what did you see?

BOB. I *saw* a knife.

Other children take their turns in similar manner.

At another time the game may be varied by having the children "take a peep" through a window.

COLORS

(Practice with *isn't*)

One child, Tom, is told to think of a color. The game proceeds as follows:

TOM. I am thinking of a color.

EDNA. Is it the color of Mary's dress?

TOM. No, it *isn't* red.

GRACE. Is it the color of this crayon?

TOM. No, it *isn't* green.

GEORGE. Is it the color of the sky?

This is the right color, *blue,* and instead of answering, Tom claps his hands. The one who guessed the color now chooses a color, and the game goes on.

WHO DID IT?

(Practice with *did*)

A leader is appointed, and the leader selects a player who is "It." The player closes his eyes. The leader points to a child, and that child immediately claps his hands softly.

The player then opens his eyes, and the leader says, "Somebody clapped. Who did it?"

The player replies, "I think __?__ *did* it."

If this is the correct guess, the child named says, "Yes, I *did* it," and changes places with the player. The game then begins again.

If a wrong guess is made, the child named shakes his head but says nothing. The leader then asks the same question again. If the player does not guess after making three trials, a new player is appointed and the game proceeds.

Play the game rapidly, and change the leader after a while.

Anyone who uses the word *done* instead of *did* must play "echo." That is, another child gives the answer correctly, and the one who missed must echo it.

Similar games can be devised at the discretion of the teacher for the correction of any gross errors that a few children in her group make. The game should be simple in execution, as are the ones above; the responses should be automatic; and the game should be pursued but a few minutes and with a few children who need the practice. Otherwise, interest will lag and the game be ineffective in producing desired results.

Bibliography

CORRECT USAGE

DAWSON, MILDRED A. *Language Arts Notes,* No. 6 and *Guiding Language Learning.* World Book Company, Yonkers-on-Hudson, New York

POOLEY, ROBERT. *Teaching English Usage.* Appleton-Century-Crofts, Inc., New York 1

THE TEACHING OF SPEECH

BACKUS, OLLIE. *Speech in Education, a Guide for the Classroom Teacher.* Longmans, Green and Company, Inc., New York 3

BAKER, PAULINE. *Primer of Sounds: A Manual for Teachers.* Expression Company, Magnolia, Massachusetts (Exercises for correcting speech faults)

BARROWS, S. T., and HALL, K. H. *Games and Jingles for Speech Development* and *Jack in the Box*. Expression Company

CASE, I. M., and BARROWS, S. T. *Speech Drills for Children in Form of Play*. Expression Company (Exercises and games)

Department of Elementary School Principals. *The Role of Speech in the Elementary School*. National Education Association, 1201 Sixteenth Street, Northwest, Washington 6, D. C.

FINLEY, G. S. *Speech and Play*. Expression Company

National Association of the Teachers of Speech. *Guides to Speech Training in the Elementary School*. Expression Company

OGILVIE, MARDEL. *Speech in the Elementary School*. McGraw-Hill Book Company, New York 36

RASMUSSEN, CARRIE. *Speech Methods in the Elementary School*. The Ronald Press Company, New York 10

RAUBICHECK, LETITIA. *How to Teach Good Speech in the Elementary Schools*. Noble and Noble Publishers, New York 3

ROBBINS, S. D., and ROBBINS, R. S. *Correction of Speech Defects of Early Childhood*. Expression Company

SCOTT, LOUISE and THOMPSON, J. J. *Talking Time*. Webster Publishing Company, St. Louis 3

WERNER, LORNA. *Speech in the Elementary School*. Row, Peterson and Company, Evanston, Illinois

Index

148